The *Ulysses* Guide

Robert Nicholson was born in Dublin, where he now lives. He studied English Language and Literature at Trinity College, Dublin, where he was active in the Dublin University Players. Since 1978 he has been the curator of the James Joyce Museum at the Joyce Tower in Sandycove, and he lectures and writes on Joyce. He has also been curator of the Dublin Writers Museum since its foundation in 1991. A former chairman of the James Joyce Institute of Ireland, he is a director of the James Joyce Centre. In addition to *The Ulysses Guide* he has published *The James Joyce Daybook*.

ROBERT NICHOLSON

The *Ulysses* Guide

TOURS THROUGH JOYCE'S DUBLIN

NEW
ISLAND

THE ULYSSES GUIDE
Published June 2002
by New Island
2 Brookside
Dundrum Road
Dublin 14

First published in Great Britain in 1988
by Methuen London Ltd

No work relating the action of *Ulysses* to its locations can be complete without reference to Clive Hart and Leo Knuth's excellent *Topographical Guide to James Joyce's Ulysses*, which identifies all addresses mentioned in the book and supplies some useful comment on the timing of each chapter. I am also indebted to Danis Rose's article in the *James Joyce Quarterly*, establishing the timing of 'Nestor' and 'Proteus' and the itinerary of the latter. Other sources are listed in the bibliography.

For permission to quote extracts from *Ulysses* and other works and letters of James Joyce I am grateful to the Estate of James Joyce. For permission to reproduce photographs from the invaluable Lawrence Collection in the National Photographic Archive I am grateful to the Trustees of the National Library of Ireland. My particular thanks are due to the late Patrick Johnston, Curator of the Dublin Civic Museum, to Peter Walsh, formerly Curator of the Guinness Brewery Museum, to Clare Gray in the National Maternity Hospital, and to Con Brogan in the Photographic Unit of Dúchas, the Heritage Service, for photographs and valuable information; to Des Gunning and his successors in the James Joyce Centre, for helpful research; to Gerard O'Flaherty, Vincent Deane and other members of the James Joyce Institute of Ireland, for points of information; to the Photographic Department, Bord Failte, for assistance; and to my colleagues in Dublin Tourism for help of various kinds.

British Library Cataloguing in Publication Data. A catalogue record for this book is available from the British Library. ISBN 1 904301 01 0

New Island receives financial assistance from The Arts Council (An Chomhairle Ealaíon), Dublin, Ireland.

Typesetting by New Island Books
Printed in Great Britain by Cox & Wyman Ltd.

Contents

Illustrations

Photographs, except where otherwise stated, are reproduced by courtesy of the National Library of Ireland from the Lawrence Collection (see page 161 for reference numbers). The maps were drawn by Neil Hyslop.

A Note on the Maps

For the sake of clarity, only the most useful and essential details are included on the maps. The reader may find it helpful to study an Ordnance Survey street map of Dublin for additional information on street names and peripheral detail. The principal route on each map is indicated with a bold line, while a broken line signifies a detour or link route. Alternate arrows pointing in opposite directions indicate that this part of the route is retraced in reverse.

Introduction

The Guide

When James Joyce wrote *Ulysses*, he did so with a copy of Thom's Dublin Directory beside him and a precise idea in his head of the location of every action described in the book. The city of Dublin, more than any scholarly work of reference, is the most valuable document we have to help us appreciate the intricate craftsmanship of *Ulysses*. To follow the steps of Leopold Bloom, Stephen Dedalus and their fellow-Dubliners from one landmark to the next has become an act, not merely of study, but of homage. It is, in effect, a sort of pilgrimage.

This guide is intended to enable pilgrims, be they scholars, students or ordinary readers, to follow the action of *Ulysses* as near as possible to the locations in which it is set. To facilitate the traveller it is arranged on an area-by-area basis rather than taking the episodes in sequence. The eight itineraries, which vary in length from one to two hours, occasionally overlap, and indications are given of how to link one route with others nearby. All are designed to be followed on foot except those of the funeral procession (Tour 2) and the viceregal cavalcade (Tour 7). Some of them begin or end conveniently near to a DART station. At certain points detours or extensions are suggested to places of Joycean or general interest. For those unfortunate enough to be precluded by distance or lack of mobility from a physical act of exploration, this book may still help with the visualisation of the time and space within which Joyce's characters move.

Incorporated in the guide is an outline of the action of *Ulysses* as it is presented in each episode. It concentrates on the activities and movements of the characters throughout the day that is described (as distinct from memories, imaginings and ideas) and is, of course, intended neither as a substitute for, nor as an interpretation of, *Ulysses* itself. Page numbers in the margin refer to the standard Corrected Text of *Ulysses* (see Appendix II), but the guide may be followed using any edition of the novel.

There are many popular misconceptions about *Ulysses*, one of them being that the book describes a walk by Leopold Bloom which can be followed continuously from one chapter to the next like some sort of tourist trail. Bloom's day is no stroll. He covers a total of about eight miles on foot and a further ten by tram, train and horse-drawn vehicle. Of certain periods of the day there is no definite account at all, and much occurs between chapters which is simply not described. The guide fills in these gaps as far as possible, and a table is appended charting the known movements of Bloom and Stephen over the course of the day.

Finally, there is one puzzle in *Ulysses* which this guide makes no attempt to solve, namely how to 'cross Dublin without passing a pub'. Maybe you will be in one when you read this.

The Changing City

Since 1904 (and even since 1988 when this guide first appeared) Dublin has altered considerably. Buildings have gone, streets have been renamed, and shops and businesses continue to change hands. Some – but only a part – of this transformation is due to the destruction caused by the Easter Rising of 1916, the War of Independence which followed, and the Civil War of 1922–3. The ravages of these events were confined to certain streets and public buildings, some of which have been restored to their original appearance. Much more widespread is the effect of the gradual removal of old houses, sometimes piecemeal and sometimes by entire blocks, which has been taking place increasingly – and especially during the booms of the 1960s and the 1990s – to make way for new property development. Many old buildings which have been preserved have also been freshened up and deprived of the shabbiness which characteristic of Joyce's Dublin.

In Bloom's time the streets were laid with cobbles or setts; main thoroughfares had tram-tracks, standards and overhead cables (which may return soon in some form); motor cars were a rarity (only one appears in *Ulysses*) and most people walked, cycled or took the tram. Without the roar and fumes of present-day motor traffic, it was possible to converse in the street as so many of Joyce's characters do, and to cross the roadway at any point without the benefit of traffic lights. Horse-drawn vehicles, however, were plentiful, and the streets were presumably foul with dung, except at the established crossings, where a line of granite setts would be kept clean by sweepers. Dublin was lit by gas; façades were not obscured by plastic and neon signs; there were no television aerials. Shopfronts were more discreet, less flashy; most shops had awnings to shade them from the sun. Most of the city's fine stone buildings were blackened and grimy with coalsmoke. Without trees, traffic islands or painted lines, Dublin's wide streets appeared even wider. Plastic bags and bottles, parking meters, traffic notices, drink cans, bilingual street signs and burglar alarms were other unknowns.

Letterboxes were red, bearing the royal cipher VR or EviiR; now painted green, some of these older boxes may still be found here and there in Dublin. Coins of the period, particularly the large copper pennies, were still in circulation up to decimalisation in 1971 – twelve pence to the shilling, twenty shillings to the pound. The guinea, worth twenty-one shillings, was a unit frequently used for fees and prices. The pound disappeared from the Irish purse in 2002 at a rate of one euro and twenty-seven cent.

Number 7 Eccles Street has gone. Barney Kiernan's has gone, and so have the *Freeman's Journal* office and Bella Cohen's brothel. Much, however, remains – the banks, the public buildings, all the churches and nearly all the pubs mentioned in *Ulysses* are still there. Even Olhausen's the butcher's and Sweny's chemist shop still survive. Many of the original buildings have altered little, despite changes of ownership. Businesses move or disappear so frequently nowadays that street numbers are included in many of the addresses given in the Guide to aid identification.

It is easy to fall into the nostalgic trap of thinking of 'Joyce's Dublin' as a city in a golden age – a time of sepia photographs, parasols, penny tramfares and the leisurely clop of horses' hooves. What we rarely see in the old photographs are the barefoot children, the rampancy of tuberculosis and rickets, the squalor of tenement life and the infamous brothels of Nighttown. Standards of hygiene and personal cleanliness were lower. The shirt which Bloom wears throughout that hot day under his black waistcoat and funeral suit will probably be worn again the next day with the cuffs turned over and a clean detachable collar. Public toilets were of the most rudimentary kind and were not provided for women. Though the poor and the intoxicated are always with us, they were there even more in Bloom's day. 'Dear, dirty Dublin' was the provincial capital of a neglected country, and if independence, prosperity and cosmopolitanism have changed it, it is not altogether for the worse.

Those who read *Ulysses* will know that Joyce was recording not merely the Dublin of 16 June 1904, but the quality of Dublin that survives through everchanging forms. This guide provides the facts of Bloomsday; by using it the reader may also discover the enduring Dublin of then and of today.

Robert Nicholson

Ulysses: The Episodes

Tour 1
Telemachus, Nestor

Telemachus, 8 a.m.

The Sandycove Martello Tower, known as the Joyce Tower, stands on a rocky headland one mile southeast of Dun Laoghaire, off the coast road. To get there, take the train to Sandycove Station and walk down to the sea, where the Tower on Sandycove Point will be clearly visible. Cars should be parked by the harbour as the Tower is on a narrow road. Turn off Sandycove Avenue at the harbour and walk up past the distinctive white house designed as his own residence by the Irish architect Michael Scott, who also designed the present Abbey Theatre, the central bus station in Store Street and other notable public buildings. Follow the path behind the house leading to the Tower.

> They halted while Haines surveyed the tower and said at last:
> —Rather bleak in wintertime, I should say. Martello you call it?
> —Billy Pitt had them built, Buck Mulligan said, when the French were on the sea. But ours is the *omphalos*.

Coincidentally enough, the order for the building of this tower, and about thirty others of similar design around Dublin and other strategic points on the Irish coast, was dated 16 June 1804. The name 'Martello' comes from Mortella Point in Corsica, where the original

Tour 1

0 ————— ¼ Mile

tower was captured, and later copied, by the British. The expected Napoleonic invasion, however, never took place, and most of the towers were demilitarised in 1867. The Sandycove Tower was one of those retained, along with the nearby battery where frequent artillery practice was a source of discomfort, according to Weston St John Joyce (no relative), to nearby residents whose windows were shattered by the concussions.

To their relief the positions were demilitarised in 1900, and in 1904 the Tower was available for rent at the sum of £8 a year. The letting was taken by Joyce's friend and the model for Buck Mulligan, Oliver St John Gogarty, in August 1904. Gogarty's plan was to establish

1. Sandycove Point in 1904. A rare photograph from *The Neighbourhood of Dublin*, looking eastwards from the coast road. The ladder may be seen beneath the door of the tower, and the structure visible to the left of the tower, behind the rooftop, was an outdoor privy.

2. Sandycove Point in 1904: A map from the lease signed by Oliver Gogarty. The dotted line around the Tower and Battery shows the War Department boundary line with its boundary stones. The 'creek' of the bathing place can be seen to the right of the battery.

the Tower as an *omphalos* or new Delphi where he could invite other young writers and kindred spirits to join him in the preaching of a modern Hellenism and more convivial pursuits. James Joyce, who arrived on 9 September, was probably more interested in having a roof over his head. His friendship with Gogarty was already cooling and he left precipitately during the night of 14-15 September, never to return.

Gogarty stayed in the Tower regularly, and continued to pay rent up to 1925. Many literary friends visited him there, including George Russell ('AE') who painted a picture on the roof, Padraic Colum, Seamus O'Sullivan, Arthur Griffith and possibly also W. B. Yeats, who was reluctantly persuaded to take a swim in the Forty Foot. The Tower might well be known now as 'Gogarty's Tower', had Joyce not used it as the setting for the opening of *Ulysses*. His implication that he himself had paid the rent effectively meant that he stole the Tower for posterity.

The James Joyce Museum, run by the Joyce Tower Society, was officially opened by Sylvia Beach, the publisher of *Ulysses*, on Bloomsday 1962. It is now owned and run by Dublin Tourism and is open daily from April to October (Monday-Saturday 10 a.m.–1 p.m., 2 p.m. –5 p.m.; Sunday 2 p.m.–6 p.m.) and by arrangement during the rest of the year (telephone the Joyce Tower 2809265 or the Dublin Writers Museum 8722077). The modern exhibition hall and entrance were added in 1978.

Pay admission at the entrance desk and go inside the Tower. At the back of the gunpowder magazine in the base is a narrow spiral staircase leading up to the top of the tower, where *Ulysses* begins.

3   'Stately, plump Buck Mulligan came from the stair-head, bearing a bowl of lather on which a mirror and a razor lay crossed. A yellow dressinggown, ungirdled, was sustained gently behind him on the mild morning air.' Around the central gunrest, which Mulligan mounts for

his parody of the Mass, and the step beneath the parapet run two rails which supported a gun carriage, swivelling from the pivot in the centre.

Stephen Dedalus, 'displeased and sleepy', follows Mulligan from the stairs and watches as he anticipates the whistle of the departing mailboat. 'Chrysostomos', the word which occurs to Stephen as he observes the gold fillings in Mulligan's teeth gleaming in the sunlight, means 'golden-mouthed', a reference to St John Chrysostom who was an early father of the Church and, appositely enough, a namesake of Mulligan and his original, Gogarty, who both have 'St John' as a middle name.

4 While Mulligan shaves, he and Stephen talk about their companion Haines and his nightmare about a black panther. Haines's real-life counterpart was Gogarty's Anglo-Irish friend Samuel Chenevix Trench, and Joyce, as we shall see, had good cause to remember the nightmare. Mulligan then calls Stephen to look at 'The snotgreen sea. The scrotumtightening sea.'

5 'Stephen stood up and went over to the parapet. Leaning on it he looked down on the water and on the mailboat clearing the harbourmouth of Kingstown.' Kingstown, named to celebrate the departure of King George IV in 1821, reverted to its original name of Dun Laoghaire with the coming of Irish independence in 1922. To the east can be seen the Muglins, a small island with a beacon, and on the next point at Bullock is another Martello tower of almost identical design. To the north, on the far side of the bay, is Howth Head, where Bloom proposed to Molly. Nearby on Sandycove Point is the half-moon battery built with the Tower, beside the Forty Foot bathing place. According to Thom's Directory, most of the houses presently on Sandycove Point were there in Joyce's time. Stephen, however, can only look at 'the ring of bay and skyline' and compare it in his mind to the bowl into which his dying mother had vomited.

6 Mulligan's teasing about his appearance only makes his mood worse as they walk around the Tower arm in arm.

7 'They halted, looking towards the blunt cape of Bray Head that lay on the water like the snout of a sleeping whale.' Bray Head is not, in fact, visible from the Tower – it is to the south beyond Killiney, whose hill with an obelisk is on the skyline – and scholars continue to agonise over whether this is a genuine slip or a deliberate error. Some diehards have drawn comfort from the possibility that the word 'towards' does not necessarily mean that they were looking *at* the Head.

8 Following his argument with Stephen, Mulligan goes downstairs, leaving Stephen to brood alone while the sun, by now somewhere over the Muglins, disappears
9 behind a cloud. His reverie about his mother reaches an anguished climax just as Mulligan returns to bid him to breakfast.

10 Stephen descends halfway down the stairs to enter 'the gloomy doomed livingroom of the tower'. To the left is the fireplace between the two window shafts (called 'barbacans' by Joyce); to the right is the heavy door opened by Haines to let in 'welcome light and bright air' from the sunny side of the building. It is unused now, and the huge key is on display downstairs. None of the original furniture (mainly supplied by Gogarty from his family home in Parnell Square) remains, but the room has now been refurnished from the evidence of contemporary documents to give an impression of the scene as it was at the time, with a shelf around the walls, a small cooking range and beds in the corners. The floor was in fact wooden rather than 'flagged', and Haines's hammock was probably Joyce's invention as there was nothing to sling it from.

It was here, on the night of 14 September 1904, that Joyce, Gogarty and Trench were sleeping when Trench had a nightmare about a black panther which he dreamed was crouching in the fireplace. Half-waking, he reached for a gun and loosed off a couple of shots to scare the beast away before going back to sleep. Gogarty promptly confiscated the gun. 'Leave the menagerie to me,' he said when Trench's nightmare returned, and fired the remaining bullets at the saucepans over Joyce's head. Joyce leapt out of bed, flung on his clothes and left the Tower immediately. He walked all the way into Dublin and appeared at the National Library at opening time. He never returned to the Tower, and the following evening he and Nora Barnacle made their decision to leave Ireland.

The big door was the only way in and out of the Tower, and was approached by a step ladder attached to 11 the outside wall. As the three men begin their breakfast Haines sees the old woman coming with the milk, and they have time to exchange a page of dialogue before she reaches the top of the ladder.

The doorway was darkened by an entering form.
—The milk, sir!

12 Haines, anxious to try out his Irish on a native, speaks to her in Gaelic which Joyce does not attempt to reproduce. Haines's original, Trench, was a keen student of the Gaelic Revival and took every opportunity to air his Connemara Gaelic, which was unfortunately marred by a strong Oxford accent.

13 The milkwoman is paid her bill (somewhat reluctantly) by Mulligan and leaves. Mulligan, obviously hopeful of getting money or drink from his friends, urges Stephen to 'Hurry out to your school kip and bring us 14 back some money' and encourages Haines to add Stephen's Hamlet theory to his collection of Irish studies. Stephen embarrasses him by asking tactlessly 'Would I make any money by it?'

15   Mulligan gets dressed and the three leave the Tower to walk to the Forty Foot. Before following their path, it is worth lingering in the Tower to view the collection, which includes several of Joyce's possessions and manuscript items, first editions of *Ulysses* and other works, and all sorts of photographs, paintings and miscellaneous Joyceana. Joyce's guitar, waistcoat and travelling trunk may be seen, and one of the two death masks made by the sculptor Paul Speck in Zürich. Among the *Ulysses* trivia are a Plumtree's Potted Meat pot and an original photograph of Throwaway, the outsider which won the Ascot Gold Cup and indirectly led to Bloom's hasty departure from Barney Kiernan's. At the entrance is a bookshop stocking Joyce's works, biographies and studies, recordings, cards, posters and prints.

    Leaving the museum, turn left down the path along
16 the top of the cliff, where Mulligan chants his 'ballad of Joking Jesus' on the way to the bathing place.

17   Stephen follows with Haines, foreseeing correctly that Mulligan will obtain the key from him and prevent him returning to the Tower. He explains to Haines how he is the servant of two masters – Britain and the Roman Catholic Church – and a third 'who wants me for odd jobs'; this last, though unspecified, is probably Irish nationalism. In his mind he has a vision of the Church and its banishment of all those who dared contest its dogmas.

18   They followed the winding path down to the creek. Buck Mulligan stood on a stone, in shirtsleeves, his unclipped tie rippling over his shoulder. A young man clinging to a spur of rock near him, moved slowly frogwise his green legs in the deep jelly of the water.

    The sign at the entrance to the bathing place once read, ambiguously, 'FORTY FOOT GENTLEMEN ONLY'. The latest wisdom on the mysterious origins of the name suggests that an offshore fishing ground gave the title to what became known as the Forty Foot Hole. The bathing place itself is only half that depth and has a long and colourful history. Probably established as a men's bathing place by the soldiers of the battery garrison in the early 1800s, it was maintained by regular bathers who in 1880 formed the Sandycove Bathers' Association. The granite screening wall protecting bathers from the east wind and the public gaze was built in the 1890s, while the concrete shelters, erected in 1969, replaced a Victorian structure on the same spot. Still famous all year round for its nude bathers, the Forty Foot has nonetheless been blithely used by both sexes since the 1970s, and the sign describing it as a 'Gentlemen's Bathing Place' merely refers to the fact that the Sandycove Bathers' Association, which maintains it for the use of the public, remains by constitution an all-male body.

19   As Stephen expected, Mulligan demands the key.

'—And twopence, he said, for a pint. Throw it here.' Mulligan and Haines arrange to meet him again at the Ship pub, where presumably he will be expected to buy them drink. He leaves them and walks back up the path on his way to Dalkey.

The most direct route, and the one which Stephen probably took, goes by way of Sandycove Avenue East and left along Breffni Road and Ulverton Road, passing Bullock Castle on the left. The castle, built in the thirteenth century, dates from the time when Bullock Harbour was the principal port of entry to Dublin for traders from abroad. Several castles in this area guarded the port and the lands of rich monasteries round about. The castle is now attached to Our Lady's Manor, a home for elderly people.

At the far end of Ulverton Road is the village of Dalkey, which in Joyce's day was the last stop on the tramline from Dublin. Dalkey has been celebrated by two later Irish writers, Flann O'Brien and Hugh Leonard.

Flann O'Brien's comic novel *The Dalkey Archive* (1964) involves a demented scientist named De Selby who plans to destroy the world with a patent substance known as DMP; also featured is James Joyce, who is discovered alive and well and claiming that *Ulysses* was a smutty book compiled under his name by a ghostwriter. Hugh Leonard's plays *Da* (1973) and *A Life* (1980) and his autobiography *Home Before Night* (1979) lovingly recreate the Dalkey of his childhood in the 1930s. A Heritage Centre in the castle in the main street tells the story of Dalkey – including its Joycean connection and other literary links – through exhibits, images and information panels. A visit to the battlements provides a view of the local topography. From April to October the Centre is open every day except Monday, and for the rest of the year it is open at weekends and public holidays.

Stephen's route continues up Dalkey Avenue as far as the corner with Old Quarry on the right.

Nestor, 9.45 a.m.

20 —You, Cochrane, what city sent for him?
—Tarentum, sir.

On the corner of Dalkey Avenue and Old Quarry, just a mile from the Tower, is a large very rambling house named 'Summerfield'. It was once the home of the poet Denis Florence McCarthy (1817-82), whose *Poetical Works* are among the volumes on Bloom's bookshelf (p.582). McCarthy was given to begetting children as well as verses, and the multiple extensions to the house were added as his family grew.

In 1904 part of the house was used by the Clifton School, run by Mr Deasy's original, Francis Irwin, where Joyce taught for a short while. It is convenient to imagine that the handsome porch was the one referred to by Joyce, that the playfield was situated on the tennis court behind the trees to the right of the gate, and that the stone pillars once bore 'lions couchant'. In fact, the school-house was at the other end of the building, in the section now called 'Greenbanks' with a separate gate on Old Quarry. The playfield was where Old Quarry road is now, but of porch, path, pillars and trees there is no sign on this side. The house and grounds are private.

As the opening episode was imbued with religion, so this one is preoccupied with history. Stephen is teaching history to a class of boys whose names – Cochrane, Armstrong, Talbot and so on – reflect their background. They are all of wealthy middle-class 'West British' families, Protestant probably and more English than Irish. 'Welloff people, proud that their eldest son was in the navy. Vico road, Dalkey.'

21 Neither Stephen nor his pupils are particularly interested in the lesson, and they switch to English and
22 a passage from Milton's *Lycidas*. When the lesson ends he asks them a riddle which they cannot answer and to which the solution is a baffling one:

> Stephen, his throat itching, answered:
> —The fox burying his grandmother under a hollybush.
> He stood up and gave a shout of nervous laughter to which their cries echoed dismay.

As countless Joyce scholars have skirted quietly round this one it seems clear that the boys were not expected to understand it either.

23 The boys leave for hockey and Stephen stays to help Sargent
24 with his sums before joining Mr Deasy in his study to get
25 paid. In the study, which resembles a little museum with its
26 cases of exhibits and curios, the theme of history dominates their conversation. Mr Deasy is proud of his unionist background and the traditions inherited from the English; Stephen thinks of it as a pageant of bigotry and violence.

27 Mr Deasy finishes a letter for the newspapers which he wishes Stephen to pass on to *The Evening Telegraph*. It proposes a solution to the foot-and-mouth disease and 28 is phrased in a series of time-worn clichés. He then delivers a diatribe against the Jews which prompts a direct comparison of their views of history. To Stephen, it 'is a nightmare from which I am trying to awake'. For Mr Deasy, 'All human history moves towards one great goal, the manifestation of God.'

29 Stephen takes his leave of Mr Deasy, and has got as 30 far as the road when Deasy follows him with a final word:

—Ireland, they say, has the honour of being the only country which never persecuted the jews. Do you know that? No. And do you know why?

He frowned sternly on the bright air.

—Why, sir? Stephen asked, beginning to smile.

—Because she never let them in, Mr Deasy said solemnly.

Leaving the school, Stephen in all probability walks to Dalkey Station via Dalkey Avenue and Cunningham Road, and takes the train to Lansdowne Road Station. From here he would turn right along Lansdowne Road and Newbridge Avenue (where *Hades* begins) to Sandymount Road, where he walked down Leahy's Terrace to the sea. Tour 2a begins at this point.

Tour 2
Nausikaa, Proteus
Hades, Wandering Rocks (vii, iv)

Stephen Dedalus probably arrives on the train from Dalkey at Lansdowne Road Station just opposite the celebrated rugby ground. James Joyce was living quite near this station in June 1904, at rented rooms in 60 Shelbourne Road, just west of the railway line.

Turn right on leaving the station and follow Lansdowne Road across the River Dodder. Taking the most direct route towards the beach would have brought Stephen along the next road to the left, Newbridge Avenue, and past No. 9 on the left hand side, where, a short while later, the mourners were to gather in the coaches to follow Paddy Dignam on his last journey. Tour 2b, along the funeral route, starts from this point. To follow Tour 2a, continue across Tritonville Road and along Sandymount Road as far as Leahy's Terrace.

2a *Nausikaa*, 8.25 p.m.

284   The summer evening had begun to fold the world in its mysterious embrace. Far away in the west the sun was setting and the last glow of all too fleeting day lingered lovingly on sea and strand …

Mr Bloom, who at this stage of the story was last seen leaving Barney Kiernan's at high speed with the citizen's dog in hot pursuit, has spent the past couple of hours

Tour 2a

0   ¼ Mile

visiting Paddy Dignam's widow in Newbridge Avenue. Afterwards he makes his way, presumably by Leahy's Terrace, to the beach. It is now almost sunset, which took place at 8.27 p.m.

In 1904 the present Beach Road did not exist. Leahy's Terrace was shorter than it is now, stretching about as

3. The Star of the Sea Church, Sandymount. Five trees, no longer young, now stand alongside the railings of Leahy's Terrace in the foreground. On the extreme left of the picture can just be seen the gap in the wall at the top of the steps leading to the strand.

far as the wall of Cosy Lodge, and ended in a set of steps leading down to the beach. All of the strand between Beach Road and Pigeonhouse Road has since been reclaimed and built on, making it difficult to locate precisely any of the activities described in this area. Press on, however, across Beach Road and over the low wall on the other side.

It seems clear that this chapter is set opposite Leahy's Terrace, within sight of the church of St Mary, Star of the Sea, and close enough to hear the singing inside. Gerty MacDowell, Cissy Caffrey and Edy Boardman are seated here on the rocks with baby Boardman in his pram and the twins Jacky and Tommy Caffrey at work on a sandcastle.

285   '... and Master Tommy would have it right go wrong that it was to be architecturally improved by a frontdoor like the Martello tower had.' The Martello tower in question, similar in pattern to the one in Sandycove, would probably be the Sandymount Tower, some dis-

tance away just round the corner of the shore on Strand Road.

The first half of the episode is told from the point of view of Gerty MacDowell, in what Joyce described to his friend Frank Budgen as 'a namby-pamby jammy marmalady drawersy (alto là!) style with effects of incense, mariolatry, masturbation, stewed cockles, painter's palette, chitchat, circumlocutions, etc. etc.' It reads in the same way as the cheap romantic magazines which obviously take up a large part of Gerty's reading time.

286 As the heroine, she is described in detail both in
287 appearance and in dress. 'Gerty was dressed simply but with the instinctive taste of a votary of Dame Fashion ...'
288 These details extend as far as her undergarments, a subject for which Joyce had a special affection.

289   Gerty's reverie of romance is interrupted by Tommy Caffrey's bold behaviour and the remarks of her companions.

290   —I'd like to give him something, she said, so I would, where I won't say.

    —On the beeoteetom, laughed Cissy merrily. Gerty MacDowell bent down her head and crimsoned at the idea of Cissy saying an unladylike thing like that out loud she'd be ashamed of her life to say, flushing a deep rosy red, and Edy Boardman said she was sure the gentleman opposite heard what she said.

291   The gentleman opposite turns out to be Leopold Bloom, who participates more actively soon afterwards
292 when Jacky Caffrey kicks the ball towards him; he throws it back and it lands at Gerty's feet. She looks at him and
293 their eyes meet. 'And while she gazed her heart went pitapat. Yes, it was her he was looking at, and there was meaning in his look.'

294   The background to their exchange is the Benediction
295 in the Star of the Sea church nearby. Gerty swings her

foot in time to the *Tantum Ergo*, showing off her stockings, and realises 'that she had raised the devil in him'. Bloom's hand is in his pocket and he removes it nervously when Cissy Caffrey approaches to ask him the time. It is getting dark. 'Edy began to get ready to go and it was high time for her [...] because it was a long way along the strand to where there was the place to push up the pushcar...'

296

Access to the beach from the higher shore was limited to a number of points where roads or public land met the beach. The steps from Leahy's Terrace were unsuitable for a pushcar so a gentler slope had to be found, possibly in the direction of Bath Street.

Cissy and Edy get the children ready to go. 'And she could see far away the lights of the lighthouses so picturesque...' The lighthouses, now out of view behind trees and buildings, include the Bailey lighthouse on Howth Head, the Poolbeg lighthouse on the South Wall and the lighthouses on Dun Laoghaire harbour to the southeast.

297
298

As they prepare to leave, the twins see the fireworks shooting up into the sky behind the church, from the bazaar in Ballsbridge to the southwest. Everyone runs down the strand for a better view, except for Gerty, who remains behind, aware that Bloom is gazing at her. 'His hands and face were working and a tremour went over her'. Leaning back to look at the fireworks, she knowingly reveals her legs to him.

299

As a Roman candle flies over the trees Gerty leans further back, displaying 'her other things too, nainsook knickers, the fabric that caresses the skin'. Bloom is given 'a full view high up above her knee' and can contain himself no longer. The fireworks express his sensations. 'And then a rocket sprang and bang shot blind blank and O! Then the Roman candle burst and it was like a sigh of O! and everyone cried O! O! in raptures and it gushed

300

out of it a stream of rain gold hair threads and they shed
and ah! they were all greeny dewy stars falling with
golden, O so lovely, O, soft, sweet, soft!'

301   Cissy calls Gerty and she rises to go. 'She walked with
a certain quiet dignity characteristic of her but with care
and very slowly because – because Gerty MacDowell
was...

'Tight boots? No. She's lame. O!'

Joyce, no doubt with tongue in cheek, labelled the
technique of this chapter 'Tumescence and detum-
escence'. Everything mounts up to a climax in a grand
explosion; deflation swiftly follows, beginning with the
revelation of Gerty's defect and the switch from her
302 thoughts to Bloom's point of view. He is left alone,
303 thinking about the ways of women and recomposing his
304 wet shirt. 'My fireworks. Up like a rocket, down like a
305 stick'. Thoughts of women put him in mind of babies
and he reminds himself to visit Mrs Purefoy in the
306 maternity hospital. Some of Gerty's perfume lingers in
the air. 'What is it? Heliotrope? No. Hyacinth? Hm.
Roses, I think. She'd like scent of that kind. Sweet and
307 cheap: soon sour.' He muses about perfume and personal
odours and smells himself. 'Almonds or. No. Lemons it
is. Ah no, that's the soap.'

308   His eye is caught by the flashing of the Bailey
lighthouse, and he recalls proposing to Molly on Howth
Head. 'Where we. The rhododendrons.' Watching the
309 bat flying about, he thinks sleepily about animals,
310 migrating birds and sailors. 'A last lonely candle' explodes
over the bazaar as nine o'clock approaches. On the shore,
the postman does his round, the lamplighter lights the
gaslight outside the church, and a newsboy circulates
with the *Evening Telegraph*, attracting the attention of
someone in the Dignam house, probably Master Patrick
Dignam, who was looking forward on page 206 to seeing
the account of the funeral in the paper.

Joyce was particular enough about his details to write a letter to his Aunt Josephine Murray (Aunt Sara's original) asking 'whether there are trees (and of what kind) behind the Star of the Sea church in Sandymount visible from the shore'.

Another light twinkles at him, from the Kish lightship far out on the horizon. It has since been replaced by a permanent lighthouse, which was built in Dun Laoghaire harbour and towed out to be sunk in position on the sandbank.

311   Tired, Mr Bloom considers his plans. 'Go home. Too late for *Leah*. *Lily of Killarney*. No. Might be still up. Call to the hospital to see. Hope she's over. Long day I've had.'

312   Finding a bit of stick, he idly starts to write a message in the sand for Gerty in case she comes that way again:

313   'I… AM. A.…', then stops and rubs it out. The noise of the cuckoo clock striking nine in the priest's house as the chapter ends suggests that 'CUCKOLD' is the word he left unwritten. Meanwhile Bloom has allowed himself to nod off for a few minutes. Later he will leave the beach and take the tram as far as Holles Street for his intended visit to Mrs Purefoy.

Proteus, 10.40 a.m.

31   Ineluctable modality of the visible: at least that if no more, thought through my eyes. Signatures of all things I am here to read, seaspawn and seawrack, the nearing tide, that rusty boot.

We return to the morning and Stephen Dedalus, who passes on his way across the strand from Leahy's Terrace the very spot where Bloom will later come to rest. His thoughts are dominated by the theme of change, as it relates to space (the modality of the visible) and time (the modality of the audible).

The strand itself has been subject to a great deal of

change since 1904. Then, it was bounded to the north by the Pigeonhouse Road and to the west by the main drainage embankment along the edge of Ringsend Park, which was at that time in the process of construction. Now, the nearest sand is a good hundred yards away to the southeast, where a standing stone on the shore, designed by Cliodna Cussen and erected in 1983, is dedicated to James Joyce. A smaller stone aligned with it points in the direction of sunrise on the winter solstice. The nearby strand was investigated by Danis Rose, who used the evidence of its seawrack, seaspawn, shells and shingle to plot the course of Stephen's walk.[1]

Stephen is walking away from Leahy's Terrace. By the time he opens his eyes he is below the tidemark, about as far as the path now running parallel to Beach Road. The tide, approaching steadily across the flat strand, is still two hours from its full at 12.42. Looking about him, he observes the two women, the *Frauenzimmer*, who have followed him down from the terrace. 'Number one swung lourdily her midwife's bag, the other's gamp poked in 32 the beach.' Prompted by the sight of the midwife, Stephen imagines himself connected back through all humanity to Eve by a succession of navelcords. 'The cords of all link back, strandentwining cable of all flesh.'

Meanwhile he is walking approximately northwestwards, following the line of the shore. Keep walking along the footpath towards Irishtown. 'His pace slackened. Here. Am I going to Aunt Sara's or not?' Stephen is heading in the direction of his aunt's house in Strasburg Terrace in Irishtown. In his mind's eye he pictures the scene if he should visit.

I pull the wheezy bell of their shuttered cottage: and wait. They take me for a dun, peer out from a coign of vantage.
—It's Stephen, sir.

—Let him in. Let Stephen in.

His uncle Richie is the same Richie Goulding with whom Bloom dines at the Ormond Hotel later in the
33 day. 'Houses of decay, mine, his and all. You told the Clongowes gentry you had an uncle a judge and an uncle a general in the army. Come out of them, Stephen. Beauty is not there.'

34 Musing about the failure of his family and of his own aspirations, Stephen walks onward. Cross Bremen Grove to a triangular patch containing the Irish Mercantile Marine Memorial, and cross again towards the nearest of the brightly painted Corporation houses. Nicknamed 'Toytown', this development won a major European environmental award when it was built in 1982. Follow Kerlogue Road towards Ringsend Park.

> The grainy sand had gone from under his feet. His boots trod again a damp crackling mast, razorshells, squeaking pebbles …

The backdoors which he sees are probably those in the area ahead and to his left in Strand Street. Ahead, across Ringsend Park, he can see the 'wigwams' of Ringsend on the Liffey docks. 'Ringsend', wrote Weston St John Joyce in 1912, 'though now presenting a decayed and unattractive appearance, was formerly a place of considerable importance, having been nearly two hundred years in conjunction with the Pigeonhouse harbour, the principal packet station in Ireland for communication with Great Britain. The transfer of the packet service, however to Howth and Kingstown in the early part of last century, deprived Ringsend of its principal source of revenue, and consigned it henceforth to poverty and obscurity.'

'He halted. I have passed the way to aunt Sara's. Am I not going there? Seems not. No one about. He turned northeast and crossed the firmer sand towards the

Pigeonhouse.' Although Strasburg Terrace is now only a short distance ahead of Stephen, he appears to have overshot the access point – a set of steps or a ramp – leading from the beach up to the shore. The route northeast leads across the present sports ground, parallel to the boundary of Ringsend Park, in the direction of the Pigeonhouse Road. The name 'the Pigeonhouse' refers variously either to the fort or to a house standing in the grounds of the electricity power station. Originally on the site was a large strongly constructed wooden house built by the port authorities in the early eighteenth century to hold stores and serve as a watch house. The caretaker, a man named Pidgeon, made his fortune by developing the premises as a popular and exclusive hostelry whose name outlived both Pidgeon and the house.

35   The name reminds Stephen of a passage from Léo Taxil's blasphemous *La Vie de Jésus*, and in turn of his Paris friend Patrice Egan who told him about it. He recalls his year in Paris and his return, summoned by

> a blue French telegram, curiosity to show:
> —Nother dying come home Father.

The 'misprint' was restored only in the Corrected Text. 'His feet marched in sudden proud rhythm over the sand furrows, along by the boulders of the south wall. He stared at them proudly, piled stone mammoth skulls. Gold light on sea, on sand, on boulders.' Cross Pine Road and follow the footpath which runs along the boundary below the pumping station. This is the route that Stephen takes alongside the boulders of the south wall, while he

36 thinks of Paris and Patrice's father Kevin Egan, the exiled
37 Fenian. This leads him directly towards the sea and he soon stops when his feet begin to sink in the wet sand. 'Turning, he scanned the shore south, his feet sinking again slowly in new sockets. The cold domed room of

the tower waits.' The Sandycove Tower is out of sight beyond Dun Laoghaire, but Stephen's thoughts may have been prompted by the sight of the similar tower on the other side of the strand. Now, of course, the entire view is obscured by the nearby houses.

'The flood is following me. I can watch it flow past from here. Get back then by the Poolbeg road to the strand there. He climbed over the sedge and eely oarweeds and sat on a stool of rock, resting his ashplant in a grike.' How far along the edge of the beach Stephen has walked is uncertain, but it is unlikely in the limited time span of this episode that he has got much further than the point where Pine Road now meets Bremen Grove, south of the old coastguard station which stands nearby. Beyond here the original coastline is lost under new roads and a fenced-off field. Behind Stephen as he sits is the long mole running out to the Pigeonhouse. In front of him he sees a dead dog and a sunken boat; approaching from the distance he sees a live dog and, further off, two figures whom he takes at first for the two midwives until he

38 realises that the dog belongs to them. Gradually they come near enough for him to distinguish 'A woman and a man. I see her skirties. Pinned up, I bet.' He sees from their activities that they are cocklepickers. This area, as Weston St John Joyce noted, 'was at one time noted for its cockles and shrimps'. The shrimps disappeared after the hard winter of 1741. 'The cockles, however, still remain for those who have the courage to eat them, and occasionally yield a rich harvest to the professional cocklepickers.'

39 The dog passes nearby and digs in the sand, its claws reminding Stephen of a panther and Haines's nightmare; he then recalls his own dream: 'Open hallway. Street of harlots. Remember, Haroun al Raschid. I am almosting it. That man led me, spoke. I was not afraid. The melon he had he held against my face...'

The cocklepickers pass, 'the ruffian and his strolling mort', and Stephen thinks of a verse written in the 'rogues' 40 rum lingo' of these gypsy folk. A moment later a poem of his own (borrowed, it must be admitted, from Douglas Hyde) begins to form in his mind.

He comes, pale vampire, through storm his eyes, his bat sails bloodying the sea, mouth to her mouth's kiss.

Hunting in his pockets for paper, he finds Deasy's letter and tears off the blank end on which to write the 41 poem. When it is finished, he lies back contemplating the toes of his borrowed boots, and notices the rising tide flowing in from Cock Lake, a pool out in the Strand. 'In long lassoes from the Cock Lake the water flowed full, covering greengoldenly lagoons of sand, rising, flowing. My ashplant will float away. I shall wait. No, they will pass on, passing, chafing against the low rocks, swirling, passing. Better get this job over quick. Listen; a fourworded wavespeech: seesoo, hrss, rsseeiss, ooos.'

The 'wavespeech' reproduces the sound of a wave breaking, spreading and receding back across the flat strand; though some scholars have conjectured that Stephen has stood up and is taking the opportunity to urinate. Looking at the water, his thoughts turn to the drowned man, 'Bag of corpsegas sopping in foul brine,' 42 and the 'seachange' he is undergoing. Finally he takes his ashplant, preparing to go. He has left his handkerchief in the Tower, and picks his nose rather than blowing it. Looking behind him over the road, he sees the 'high spars of a threemaster', moving up the Liffey into the port of Dublin, 'a silent ship'.

Stephen plans to return by going up onto 'the Poolbeg Road', i.e. the Pigeonhouse Road which also leads out along the two-mile pier to the lighthouse which Joyce elsewhere calls 'the Poolbeg flasher'. Now painted bright red, it was black in 1904. From the road, he can follow the directions advised by Weston St John Joyce. 'Returning along the Wall, we take the turn on the left along the Rathmines and Pembroke Main Drain embankment [i.e. along the edge of Ringsend Park], which has reclaimed from the sea a considerable tract now being laid out as a public park.' (Nowadays it is not so easy to follow this route. Instead, turn back along the path you are on directly towards the boundary of the Park.)

This route is the most direct one to lead him to Irishtown via Strand Street and the Irishtown Road. It also happens to bring him straight past Aunt Sara's front door in Strasburg Terrace. He reaches Irishtown in time to be spotted by Mr Bloom between Watery Lane (now Dermot O'Hurley Avenue) and the library on the corner. From here he walks into town in the trail of the funeral procession, stopping in College Green to send a telegram to Mulligan before going on to the newspaper office.

To follow the entire route of the funeral cortège, start by returning from Strasburg Terrace to 9 Newbridge Avenue and then provide yourself with a carriage or other vehicle.

2b *Hades*, 11 a.m.

72 Martin Cunningham, first, poked his silkhatted head into the creaking carriage and, entering deftly, seated himself.

With the introduction of one-way traffic systems it is no longer possible to follow the entire route of the funeral procession by car or horse-drawn cab. Ideally, it may be done by bicycle, dismounting to follow one-way streets on foot where they occur.

The hearse and carriages leave from outside 9 Newbridge Avenue and turn left onto the cobbles of the tramline along Tritonville Road. Carole Brown and Leo Knuth, in a special study of this chapter,[2] have worked

Tour 2b

out that in all likelihood Bloom is sitting on the left hand side, facing forward. Opposite him is Simon Dedalus, facing rearwards. Jack Power is sitting beside Bloom and Martin Cunningham is in the seat diagonally opposite.

—What way is he taking us? Mr Power asked through both windows.

—Irishtown, Martin Cunningham said. Ringsend, Brunswick street.

4. Irishtown Road. Rattling along this 'cobbled causeway', the funeral carriages pass Dodder Terrace here on the left. At the junction with Bath Street a little further on, the road veers left into Irishtown. Behind the houses in the background, Ringsend Park is under construction.

73   Proceeding along Irishtown Road into Ringsend, the carriage passes Watery Lane (now Dermot O'Hurley Avenue) on the left and then swerves from the tramtrack to travel to the left of the island where a public library now stands. This was probably to avoid the major road works consequent upon the laying down of the new main drainage scheme. At this point 'Mr Bloom at gaze saw a lithe young man, clad in mourning, a wide hat.' He recognises Stephen Dedalus and points him out to his father.

74   The carriage turns the corner onto Ringsend Road and crosses the humpbacked bridge over the Dodder. A little further on it stops.

—What's wrong?

—We're stopped.
—Where are we?
    Mr Bloom put his head out of the window.
—The grand canal, he said.

The bridge over the Grand Canal was designed to be raised to allow access to the inner canal dock, and this was presumably the reason for the brief halt. On the left beside the bridge is Boland's Mill, one of the buildings occupied by rebel troops in the Easter Rising in 1916. The commander of this stronghold, born in the same year as Joyce, was Eamon de Valera, who later became Ireland's foremost political leader. The gasworks were across the canal to the right, and the Cats' and Dogs' Home is ahead and to the left.

75 Resuming their journey, the mourners travel over the canal and along Great Brunswick Street (now Pearse
76 Street). They pass on the left St Andrew's National School and Meade's timberyard on the corner of South Cumberland Street, then the 'hazard' or cab rank beside the railway station. 'An hour ago I was passing there,' thinks Bloom.

On the right is the building formerly known as the Antient Concert Rooms, which features in Joyce's story 'A Mother' in *Dubliners*. Joyce himself sang there in a concert on 27 August 1904, sharing the bill with such notables as J. C. Doyle and the great Irish tenor John McCormack – both of whom are to take part in Blazes Boylan's concert tour with Molly Bloom. The building has been empty for some years and work is currently in progress to restore it.

Next to this is 'the bleak pulpit of saint Mark's' where Oscar Wilde was baptised in 1854. Further up the street on the left was the Queen's Theatre, now replaced by a modern office block. The Abbey theatre company took up a fifteen-year residence there in 1951 after the

5. The Crampton Memorial. This late photograph shows the back of the sculpture. On the other side, Sir Philip's bust faced up Pearse Street, towards the approaching funeral cortège.

old Abbey was destroyed by fire. On the right at No. 27, on the wall above the restored shop-front of the premises of Pearse and Sons, may be seen bas-relief portraits of the monumental sculptor's sons, the 1916 leader Patrick Pearse and his brother Willie, who lived here. The soaring florentine tower beyond it belongs to the Fire Station.

As they near Boylan's office Bloom thinks helplessly about Molly's assignation. 'He's coming in the afternoon. Her songs. Plasto's. Sir Philip Crampton's memorial fountain bust. Who was he?' The Crampton Memorial, one of Dublin's more extraordinary monuments, stood in the junction at the end of Pearse Street until its semi-collapse in 1959. Because of the botanical nature of the structure, it was popularly known as 'the Cauliflower'. It commemorated Sir Philip Crampton (1777-1858), the Irish Surgeon General. Near its place now stands a stone pillar by Cliodna Cussen, commemorating the fact that this was the original site of the 'Long Stone' erected by the Vikings.

The procession turns right along D'Olier Street (traffic nowadays must continue to Westmoreland Street), passing Blazes Boylan outside the Red Bank Restaurant on the right. The restaurant is now a hostel, Ashfield House, but careful observers may still see the carvings of lobsters and other delicacies on the wall outside.

(188)   *Wandering Rocks vii* is set in Boylan's office, believed to be the Advertising Co. Ltd. at 15 D'Olier Street, now part of the *Irish Times* office on the left next to Fleet
(189) Street. His secretary, Miss Dunne, takes a phone call from Boylan, who is ringing from Thornton's fruit shop. She takes his instructions and passes on a message: 'Mr Lenehan, yes. He said he'll be in the Ormond at four.'

Detour for drivers: keep straight on from Pearse Street along College Street, turn right along Westmoreland Street and rejoin the funeral route at O'Connell Bridge.

77   'Smith O'Brien. Someone has laid a bunch of flowers there. Woman. Must be his deathday.' The statue of William Smith O'Brien, which once stood at the junction of D'Olier Street, Westmoreland Street and O'Connell Bridge, has been moved further down O'Connell Street to stand between 'the hugecloaked Liberator's form' of Daniel O'Connell and the statue of Sir John Gray.

Passing over O'Connell Bridge, celebrated for being as wide as it is long, they proceed down O'Connell Street (formerly Sackville Street), Dublin's premier boulevard. Although the street has changed in many aspects since 1904, the two most striking changes at street level are the motor traffic (which attempts are now in hand to reduce) and the introduction of a central island running the length of the street and planted with trees. Previously the impression was of a wide open space rather than the channels of today. Outside Elvery's Elephant House, now

Kentucky Fried Chicken, on the corner of Middle Abbey
78 Street, they spot Reuben J. Dodd and a story is told about
the rescue of Dodd's son from the Liffey when he tried
to drown himself. The BBC broadcast this section of the
novel in the 1950s and thought it was a great joke when
someone claiming to be Reuben J. Dodd Junior brought
a libel suit against them. Dodd won his case.

79   'Dead side of the street this.' Bloom is looking at the
west side of O'Connell Street north of the GPO as they
approach the foundation stone of the present Parnell
Monument (the statue by Augustus Saint Gaudens was
unveiled in 1911, twenty years after Parnell's death). The
dead are so dominant in this episode that it is appropriate
to note the Gresham Hotel on the opposite side, where
Gabriel and Gretta Conroy spent the night in 'The Dead'.

Another *Dubliners* location is the Rotunda Concert
Rooms (still a music venue, but renamed the
Ambassador) where Mr Duffy met Mrs Sinico in 'A
Painful Case'. 'Two Gallants' starts here on 'the hill of
Rutland Square', now Parnell Square. Oliver Gogarty's
family home at No. 5, opposite the Gate Theatre, is
marked by a plaque.

The men in the carriage discuss the morality of
suicide; only Martin Cunningham knows that Bloom's
father poisoned himself. On their left at the top of the
hill is Findlater's Church; next door to it at 18 Parnell
Square is the Dublin Writers Museum, where Joyce's
piano is part of a fascinating collection tracing Ireland's
illustrious literary history. The cortège continues up
North Frederick Street, over Dorset Street and along
Blessington Street into Berkeley Street.

80   *Detour for drivers*: Until the current proposal to allow
traffic to go north up Parnell Square East and North
Frederick Street becomes a reality, motorists should turn
left at the Parnell Monument and take the first turn right
up Parnell Square West and Granby Row. Turn right

again onto Dorset Street, pass Blessington Street and turn left up Eccles Street to rejoin the funeral route beside the Mater Hospital. 'The *Mater Misericordiae*. Eccles Street. My house down there.'

As they turn the corner left onto the North Circular Road they are delayed by a herd of cattle being driven
81 to the docks. They drive onwards to the Phibsborough Road. 'Dunphy's corner. Mourning coaches drawn up, drowning their grief. A pause by the wayside. Tiptop position for a pub.' Dunphy's Corner is now known as Doyle's Corner, and the pub bears the grandiose name of Sir Arthur Conan Doyle, an author of Irish descent whose Sherlock Holmes stories did for London what *Ulysses* was later to do for Dublin. The carriages turn right here onto the Phibsborough Road.

Detour for motorists: *Wandering Rocks iv*. Continue to the next turn right onto St Peter's Road. The Joyce family lived on the left-hand side at No. 7 (St Peter's Terrace) in 1904, and it is apparently here that the Dedalus family is in residence.

(186)   Katey and Boody Dedalus shoved in the door of the closesteaming kitchen.
—Did you put in the books? Boody asked.

Katey and Boody have come from the pawnbroker's in Gardiner Street via Eccles Street, and are given soup by their sister Maggy.

Turn right again round Dalymount Park and rejoin the funeral route on Phibsborough Road.

82   In silence they drove along Phibsborough Road. An empty hearse trotted by, coming from the cemetery: looks relieved. Crossguns bridge: the royal canal.

The carriages cross the canal and pass the Brian Boroimhe pub. More commonly spelt Brian Boru, this ancient Irish king is another of the commemorated dead who punctuate the funeral route. He is famous for beating the Danes at the Battle of Clontarf in 1014, during which he himself was killed by a Dane who entered his tent while he was praying. Steering left for Finglas Road, they pass the Childs murder house at 36 Bengal Terrace (Mr Power wrongly points to the last house, number 38) on the right next to the graveyard. The murder of seventy-six-year-old Thomas Childs took place in September 1899; Childs's brother Samuel was charged but acquitted.

83 Finally they draw to a halt at the gate of the graveyard
84 and the mourners walk inside. 'First the stiff: then the friends of the stiff.' The cemetery is open daily from 8.30 a.m. to 5 p.m. for public visits.

Dominating the entrance to the cemetery is the O'Connell Monument, a round tower with a 'lofty cone'. To the left is the mortuary chapel, opposite to the tombs of priests and bishops and 'the cardinal's mausoleum'. The cardinal in question was Archbishop McCabe, referred to by Mr Dedalus in *A Portrait* as 'the tub of guts up in Armagh'. 'Billy with the lip' – Archbishop William Walsh – lies nearby.

Bloom meets Tom Kernan and Ned Lambert, who
85 were in the other carriage, and the mourners enter the
86 chapel for the funeral service. When it is over they follow the coffincart outside and to the left 'along a lane of sepulchres' and walk towards Dignam's grave. Where-abouts he is buried Joyce does not specify, but the probable area may be reached by walking down the cypress avenue by the chapel, turning left at the bottom,
87 and right at the next intersection. Bloom and Kernan follow Ned Lambert and John Henry Menton, Dignam's
88 employer, and they meet John O'Connell, the caretaker,
89 on the way. By the graveside Bloom looks towards the Botanic Gardens just behind the cemetery and muses
90 about the effect of the corpses on the soil. Nearby he sees the mystery mourner whose identity has intrigued Joyceans ever since. 'Now who is that lankylooking galoot

over there in the macintosh? Now who is he I'd like to know?'

91   In the silence after the coffin is lowered he thinks about his own grave nearby: 'Mine over there towards Finglas, the plot I bought. Mamma, poor mamma, and little Rudy.'

92   Joe Hynes of the *Evening Telegraph* approaches Bloom, collecting a list of names.

> —And tell us, Hynes said, do you know that fellow in the, fellow was over there in the…
> He looked around.
> —Macintosh. Yes, I saw him, Mr Bloom said. Where is he now?
> —M'Intosh, Hynes said scribbling. I don't know who he is. Is that his name?
> He moved away, looking about him.

The erratic results of Hynes's scribblings may be found on p.529.

Returning by the same route, turn right at the intersection and walk a short distance along the path. On the left is a mound surrounded by an iron railing and surmounted by a huge boulder of Wicklow granite inscribed simply PARNELL. A stone plaque reads 'The Chief's Grave'. Parnell was buried here in 1891. Mourners leaving his funeral plucked ivy leaves from the cemetery wall, and the anniversary of his death on 6 October was celebrated every year thereafter as Ivy Day.

93   Hynes and Mr Power go round this way. Just before Parnell's grave, on the opposite side of the path, is the grave of Joyce's parents. The tombstone, which stands three away from the path, was inscribed according to Joyce's own instructions after his father's death in 1931.

Mr Bloom meanwhile walks along 'by saddened angels, crosses, broken pillars, family vaults, stone hopes praying with upcast eyes, old Ireland's hearts and hands', musing over the tombstones and remembering that he will be visiting his father's grave in Ennis on 27 June, the anniversary of his death.

The centenary of Rudolph Bloom's suicide in 1986 was observed by the James Joyce Institute of Ireland, who travelled to Ennis to visit the grave. Unfortunately, as the gardener had long since stopped receiving his annual ten shillings, Rudolph's resting-place could not be found in the undergrowth.

94 'The gates glimmered in front; still open. Back to the world again. Enough of this place. Brings you a bit nearer every time. Last time I was here was Mrs Sinico's funeral.' Mrs Sinico's funeral, as we learn elsewhere, took place on 17 October 1903. The story of her death under a train at Sydney Parade Station is related in 'A Painful Case' in *Dubliners*.

95 On the way to the gates Bloom joins Martin Cunningham and John Henry Menton. He points out a dinge in

6. Glasnevin Cemetery. The picture shows the O'Connell Monument and the chapel.

Menton's hat but is treated coldly by Menton, who dislikes him. 'Chapfallen', he follows them to the gates.

It is worth staying awhile to explore the cemetery. Many of Joyce's family, friends and associates lie here, including those who appear as characters in *Ulysses* – Skin-the-Goat, Michael ('the citizen') Cusack, Father Conmee, J.P. Nannetti and others. In an unusual ceremony in 1988, an elaborate tombstone was placed on the grave of Matthew Kane, the original of Martin Cunningham, whose funeral in July 1904 after his death by drowning was attended by Joyce and his father and is therefore claimed as the original of Dignam's. Some of the most celebrated Irish men and women buried here over the past 150 years are to be found by the east side of the O'Connell Monument.

From Glasnevin the mourners return by coach to the city centre, where *Aeolus* (Tour 6) takes place. Alternatively, retrace the funeral route to Doyle's Corner, continue through the crossroads and turn right at the lights along Monck Road and Avondale Road. At the top of Avondale Road turn left to follow the North Circular Road as far as Phoenix Park to begin Tour 7.

Tour 3
Calypso, Ithaca, Penelope,
Wandering Rocks (iii, i, ii)

Calypso, 8 a.m.

45   Mr Leopold Bloom ate with relish the inner organs of beasts and fowls. He liked thick giblet soup, nutty gizzards, a stuffed roast heart, liverslices fried with crustcrumbs, fried hencods' roes. Most of all he liked grilled mutton kidneys which gave to his palate a fine tang of faintly scented urine.

Leopold Bloom's house at 7 Eccles Street, one of the most famous addresses in world literature, is now no more. It was situated on the right hand side as you approach from Dorset Street, approximately opposite No. 76. The site is now marked by a bronze plaque beside the front door of the Mater Private Hospital, with a relevant quotation from *Ithaca*. Once the residence of Joyce's friend J. F. Byrne (the 'Cranly' of *A Portrait*), it was officially listed as vacant in the 1904 Thom's Directory. In later years it became derelict and was half-demolished in 1967. In 1982 it was finally levelled to make way for the present building. Bricks and other relics are scattered throughout the Joycean world.

The houses opposite give some idea of its appearance. The kitchen, where Mr Bloom appears at breakfast, was in the basement. He prepares his wife's breakfast tray, 46 gives the cat some milk, goes upstairs to the hall beside the bedroom on the ground floor, and comes out through

Tour 3

7. The Mater Hospital, Eccles Street. Bloom's house is near the bottom of the street in the terrace on the left-hand side, which has now been replaced by the private wing of the hospital.

the front door. 'He pulled the halldoor to after him very quietly, more, till the footleaf dropped gently over the threshold, a limp lid. Looked shut.'

The footleaf, a hinged flap serving as a draught excluder, may be seen on other doors nearby or indeed on the original door of 7 Eccles Street itself, which may be inspected not very far away in the James Joyce Centre in North Great George's Street.

'He crossed to the bright side, avoiding the loose cellarflap of number seventyfive. The sun was nearing the steeple of George's church.'

The cellarflap was a heavy iron disc in the pavement covering the coalhole, through which coal deliveries could thus be made directly from the street. Some of the older Dublin cellarflaps are particularly ornate and of various styles. St George's Church in Hardwicke Place was designed by Francis Johnston in 1802, and Arthur Wellesley, the future Duke of Wellington, was married here in 1806 just before his involvement in the Peninsular War. The bells which chimed on every quarter hour of day or night have been removed to Taney Church in Dundrum, and the building, since relinquished by the Church of Ireland, is now the Temple Theatre. The spire, which has been in scaffolding for many years, is reported to be in a dangerous condition and the future will see either its removal or its reinstatement.

47 Bloom approaches Larry O'Rourke's on the corner,
48 where he turns right into Dorset Street. Recently restored to its state of Edwardian elegance after years of scruffiness, the pub is now named The Snug. He passes St Joseph's national school at No. 81-84, which now bears the name 'St Raphael's House', and enters Dlugacz's the pork butcher's between the school and Blessington Street. This establishment, of which no record exists, was apparently invented by Joyce, who mischievously named it after a Jewish acquaintance in Trieste.

49 Bloom buys a pork kidney and returns towards Eccles Street, reading a pamphlet, picked from the butcher's pile of wrapping paper, which advertises a scheme by a planter's company named Agendath Netaim to buy land
50 near Galilee. A cloud – the same one, apparently, which Stephen sees from the Tower on page 8 – covers the sun and sheds gloom on his thoughts. Further gloom awaits him at his front door. 'Two letters and a card lay on the hallfloor. He stooped and gathered them. Mrs Marion Bloom. His quickened heart slowed at once. Bold hand. Mrs Marion.' He realises that the letter to his wife is from Blazes Boylan to make an assignation – a suspicion which is borne out when Molly does not open the letter in his presence.

51 His own letter, which he glances at in the kitchen, is from his daughter Milly in Mullingar. He puts the kidney on to cook and brings Molly's breakfast upstairs. Here
52 he pauses to explain the word 'metempsychosis' which

she has found, strangely enough, in a trashy novel named *Ruby: the Pride of the Ring* (identified as a novel by Amye Reade in which, however, the word does not appear[3]).

53 Smelling the burning kidney, he hurries downstairs to
54 eat breakfast and reread Milly's letter. After breakfast he
55 goes out through the backdoor, armed with an old
56 number of *Titbits*, and heads for the outdoor lavatory in the garden rather than 'fag up the stairs to the landing'. 'Asquat on the cuckstool' he reads the prize story by Philip
57 Beaufoy before using it to wipe himself. As he emerges, the church bells chime at quarter to nine.

Soon afterwards he leaves to walk to the quays, probably by the same route which he and Stephen follow in reverse in *Ithaca*.

Ithaca, 1 a.m.

544 What parallel courses did Bloom and Stephen follow returning?

545 The itinerary described at the beginning of the episode, leading from Beresford Place via Gardiner Street, Mountjoy Square, Gardiner Place, Temple Street and Hardwicke Place to Eccles Street, may be taken as a variation from Tour 4.

The chapter, written in the form of a catechism, is at times ludicrously pedantic in style. It also supplies us with the vast bulk of the factual information that can be obtained about Bloom and, to a lesser extent, Stephen.

546 Arriving at his front door, Bloom realises that he has forgotten to transfer his latchkey to the pocket of his funeral suit (a fact of which he was aware when he went to the butcher's in the morning). 'Bloom's decision?' – 'A stratagem.' He climbs over the railings, down into the

547 area, and enters through the basement door. Stephen is brought in through the front door and down into the

548/9 kitchen. Bloom puts on the kettle, finally uses the lemon

550 soap to wash his hands, and offers Stephen a wash which

he declines ('his last bath having taken place in the month
551 of October of the preceding year'). On the dresser he
552 discovers traces of Boylan's visit: the fruit basket, a half
empty bottle of port, and 'Four polygonal fragments of
two lacerated scarlet betting tickets, numbered 8 87, 88
6.' He realises at this point the coincidences during the
day which prophesied Throwaway's victory in the Gold
Cup race.
553 Bloom makes cocoa and they drink it. We learn of
554 Bloom's early literary compositions, the relationship
555 between his age (thirty-eight) and Stephen's (twenty-two),
556–8 and other comparisons and links between them. Bloom
559 talks of his ideas for effective advertising; Stephen suggests
560 an advertisement featuring a piece of paper with 'Queen's
Hotel' written on it. Unknown to him, Bloom's father
poisoned himself in the Queen's Hotel in Ennis, of which
561 he was the proprietor. Stephen tells Bloom 'The Parable
562 of the Plums' which he related earlier in the day outside
563 the newspaper office; they discuss famous Jews and
564 compare the Jewish and Irish alphabets and languages
(of which neither of them has any practical knowledge).
565 Stephen chants 'in a modulated voice a strange legend',
566 the tale of little Harry Hughes, who has his head cut off
567 by 'a jew's daughter, all dressed in green.' Disturbed,
568–9 Bloom thinks about his own daughter Milly.
570 Bloom invites Stephen to stay overnight, but his
571 invitation is declined. He returns Stephen his money,
and they discuss the possibility of meeting for further
572 conversations and mutual instruction. They go out through
573 the backdoor into the garden and observe the clear
summer night sky, 'The heaventree of stars hung with
humid nightblue fruit.'
574 Bloom's scientific mind discards this artistic spectacle
575 and views it prosaically enough as '…an infinity render-
able equally finite by the suppositious apposition of one
or more bodies equally of the same and of different

576 magnitudes.' His contemplation of the universe is interrupted by the sight of a light in the bedroom window.

577 At Stephen's suggestion, at Bloom's instigation both, first Stephen, then Bloom, in penumbra urinated, their sides contiguous, their organs of micturition reciprocally rendered invisible by manual circumposition.

578 Bloom lets Stephen out by the door into Eccles Lane. Where he goes for the rest of the night is never even
579 stated. Alone, Bloom returns indoors, ascends the stairs and enters the living room at the front, to find that the
580 furniture has been rearranged. He uses the Agendath
581 Netaim prospectus to light a cone of incense, and notices that some of the books on the shelf are upside down. He
582-3 rearranges them, sits down and loosens his clothes.

584 The budget for 16 June 1904 is interesting. It reveals that Bloom travelled by tram from town to Sandymount after his bath, and from Sandymount to town between *Nausikaa* and *Oxen of the Sun*. More intriguingly, the account omits his trainfare to Nighttown, the ten shillings he paid on page 455 and the further shilling for the damaged lamp on page 478.

585-91 As a relaxation before retiring he lets himself think about his ultimate ambition to settle comfortably in a well-appointed residence, and about schemes to enable
592-3 him to afford it. He opens a drawer to place in it his letter from Martha Clifford, whose name and address are also in the drawer, written in a cryptogram which clearly translates as MARTHA/CLIFFORD/DOLPHINS/BARN. J. F. Byrne, a later occupant of Bloom's house, was an expert on cyphers. This drawer contains a multitude of miscellaneous objects, from cameo brooches to erotic
594 postcards. The other drawer is reserved for certificates
595 and important documents, some relating to Bloom's
596 father, whom they bring to his mind. The financial

documents are a security against a situation of poverty,
597 which can only be precluded by death or departure. The
598 possibilities of his departure are considered, including a
Missing Person advertisement with his description
('height 5 ft 9 ½ inches, full build, olive complexion').

599–600 He reviews the day briefly and, 'gathering multi-
coloured multiform multitudinous garments', goes into
601 the bedroom where he puts on his nightshirt and enters
the bed. He and Molly have their heads at opposite ends
of the bed.

What did his limbs, when gradually extended,
encounter?
New clean bedlinen, additional odours, the presence
of a human form, female, hers, the imprint of a human
form, male, not his, some crumbs, some flakes of
potted meat, recooked, which he removed.

Bloom finally finds himself able to consider Boylan's
intrusion with equanimity. He is, after all, merely one of
a series of men who have found Molly attractive. Bloom
602–3 feels no sense of having 'been outraged by the adulterous
violator'. It is, in a strange way, a victory for him.

604 He wakes Molly by a display of affection – 'He kissed
the plump mellow yellow smellow melons of her rump,
on each plump melonous hemisphere, in their mellow
605 yellow furrow' – and treats her to a carefully modified
account of the day's activities. It is only now that we learn
that Bloom and his wife have not had complete sexual
606 intercourse since before Rudy's birth more than ten years
ago, and that in recent months Molly has taken to
questioning Bloom every time he goes out.

607 Finally Bloom's thoughts melt into confusion and he
drifts off to sleep, dreaming about another traveller,
Sinbad the Sailor. 'Where?' the last question asks. The
answer is a full stop.

Penelope, 1.45 a.m.

608–44   'Yes because he never did a thing like that before as ask to get his breakfast in bed with a couple of eggs…' Molly Bloom's soliloquy, which has been seen or heard in performance more often than any other episode of *Ulysses*, begins where *Ithaca* leaves off. It is divided into eight so-called sentences and is totally unpunctuated apart from one full stop at the end of the fourth sentence and one at the end of the final sentence, ending the book. The full stop on page 624 was in fact, only 'rediscovered' in the Corrected Text, and the appropriate thesis about its significance has still to appear. Its position suggests that it acts as a central hinge of some sort.

    Because, as Frank Budgen remarks, 'her thoughts jostle one another like the citizens of an egalitarian republic', it is difficult to summarise the episode coherently. Her thoughts swirl about, returning frequently to Boylan and the events of the afternoon, but more and more consistently towards Bloom, whom she finds at turns irritating and endearing.

    Much of Molly's day can be pieced together from her thoughts. During the morning, besides rearranging the furniture, she burned a lot of old newspapers and magazines, put the remainder up in the WC, and cleared some old overcoats out of the hall (p.621). In preparation for Boylan's visit she spent 'hours dressing and perfuming and combing' (p.611). At quarter past three, when Katey and Boody Dedalus passed by and the onelegged sailor was begging in the street, she was still in a state of undress whistling 'There is a charming girl I love' in the living room (p.615). Soon afterwards the messengerboy from Thornton's arrived with the port and peaches, and 'I was just beginning to yawn with nerves thinking he was trying to make a fool of me when I knew his tattarrattat at the door' (p.615).

Whether Boylan and Molly paused to rehearse the concert programme before getting down to the main business of the afternoon is not clear. The activity in the bedroom is graphically recalled on pages 611, 617, 620, 621, 633, 638 and 641, the general impression being one of action rather than affection. At some stage they took a break to drink port and eat potted meat. '...he had all he could do to keep himself from falling asleep after the last time after we took the port and potted meat it had a fine salty taste yes...'(p.611)

Boylan also went out to buy an *Evening Telegraph* for the result of the race and came back 'swearing blazes because he lost 20 quid'. He tore up the betting tickets on the dresser where Bloom found them later.

Boylan left, slapping Molly's behind familiarly. After his departure she had a pork chop from Dlugacz's for tea and returned to bed, where she slept soundly until woken by the thunder at ten o'clock.

Boylan occupies relatively little of Molly's thoughts, which revolve mainly round her husband, day-to-day trivia and memories of her girlhood in Gibraltar, her boyfriend Harry Mulvey who kissed her under the Moorish wall, and another early lover, lieutenant Gardner. Her mind shifts from one man to another and the word 'he' can refer to two different men in one line. Her reverie is interrupted by her period – 'O jesus wait yes that thing has come on me yes now wouldn't that afflict you' – and pages 633-4 are delivered from the chamberpot. On page 637 she starts thinking about Stephen Dedalus and the possibility of his becoming a regular visitor. 'I suppose hes 20 or more Im not too old for him if hes 23 or 24'.

The unrefined Boylan is a write-off as far as romance is concerned – 'of course hes right enough in his way to pass the time as a joke' – and in the end it is Bloom that she thinks of and the day in 1888 when he proposed to

her on Howth Head. '…and I thought well as well him
as another and then I asked him with my eyes to ask
again yes and then he asked me would I yes to say yes
my mountain flower and first I put my arms around him
yes and drew him down to me so he could feel my breasts
all perfume yes and his heart was going like mad and yes
I said yes I will Yes.'

Wandering Rocks iii, 3.15 p.m.

185   A onelegged sailor crutched himself round Mac-
         Connell's corner, skirting Rabaiotti's icecream car,
         and jerked himself up Eccles Street.

The sailor has come from Gardiner Street via Dorset
Street. MacConnell's the chemist's at 112 Dorset Street
was not actually on the corner itself. He passes the
Dedalus girls and stops outside 7 Eccles Street. Molly
Bloom, inside in her underwear, flings a coin from the
window on the ground floor; the sign *Unfurnished
Apartments* refers to the rooms on the floor above.

The line referring to J. J. O'Molloy is an interpolation
of a simultaneous event taking place in Meetinghouse
Lane, setting of *WR viii* (p. 189). In a similar
interpolation on page 205, the sailor reappears in Nelson
Street, off Eccles Street.

From Eccles Street, cross Dorset Street and proceed
through Hardwicke Place past St George's Church to the
bottom of Temple Street North, where there is the
opportunity to make a detour to two particularly
interesting Joycean landmarks nearby. Turn right at the
corner to Belvedere College, the Jesuit school attended
by James Joyce from 1893 to 1898 and described in *A
Portrait of the Artist as a Young Man*. The college stands
at the head of North Great George's Street, a distinctive
Georgian thoroughfare where lived Sir Samuel Ferguson,
the poet, Sir John Pentland Mahaffy, a famous Provost
of Trinity College who associated with Oscar Wilde and

Oliver Gogarty, and John Dillon, the Irish Nationalist MP. No. 35, two-thirds of the way down on the left, was formerly the dancing academy of 'Mr Denis J Maginni, professor of dancing &c' (who appears in an interpolation near here on page 181, and later on page 208). The house, finely restored, now leads a new and exciting existence as the James Joyce Centre, which was opened to the public in 1996 as a centre for Joycean study, research and cultural activities. Visitors may take a tour, watch the audiovisual presentation, browse at will in a fascinating library of works by, about and related to Joyce, and visit the exhibition rooms or the Paul Léon Room, where the chairs and table at which Joyce worked in his friend's Paris flat in the 1930s are preserved. They may call in to the bookshop or admire the tearoom murals depicting the eighteen episodes of *Ulysses*. Some close relatives of Joyce are actively involved in the Centre and may be met there, along with passing scholars and Joycean pilgrims.

Back at Temple Street, follow Gardiner Place (where a plaque on the Dergvale Hotel commemorates Michael Cusack, founder of the Gaelic Athletic Association and model for Joyce's character 'the citizen') as far as Mountjoy Square. Opposite and to the left is St Francis Xavier's Church (scene of the retreat in 'Grace', the *Dubliners* story). Beyond the church is the presbytery from which Father Conmee emerges at five to three.

Wandering Rocks i, 2.55 p.m.

180   The superior, the very reverend John Conmee S. J. reset his smooth watch in his interior pocket as he came down the presbytery steps. Five to three. Just nice time to walk to Artane.

Father Conmee (1847-1910) was appointed Rector of Clongowes Wood College in 1885, and appears in that position in *A Portrait of the Artist as a Young Man*.

8. St Francis Xavier's Church. Father Conmee passes the church just after five to three.

He left Clongowes in 1891, the same year that Joyce did (because his father could no longer afford to pay the fees), and was later instrumental in having the Joyce boys educated for free at Belvedere (rather than suffer the awful fate of being educated with 'Paddy Stink and Micky Mud' in the Christian Brothers). In 1898 he was appointed superior of the St Francis Xavier's community in Gardiner Street, in which role he appears here.

He meets the sailor outside the convent on the corner and crosses to Mountjoy Square, where he meets the wife of Mr David Sheehy M.P. under the trees on the north side. The Sheehys were well known to Joyce, who was a frequent visitor to their home at 2 Belvidere Place. He was particularly friendly with Mary Sheehy, who later married the poet Thomas Kettle. Another sister, Hannah, married Joyce's friend Francis Skeffington, who appears as 'McCann' in *A Portrait*. Skeffington, an ardent pacifist, was arrested and summarily executed during the Easter Rising; Kettle died in the war in France. A younger brother, Eugene Sheehy, one of the boys in Belvedere, became a prominent judge. His memoir, *May it Please the Court*, contains some entertaining recollections of Joyce.

181   At the corner of Mountjoy Square he meets some schoolboys and gets one of them to post a letter in 'the red pillarbox at the corner of Fitzgibbon street'. Now gone, the pillarbox stood on the north side of the street at the corner. The Joyce family moved to Fitzgibbon Street from Blackrock in 1892; their house at No. 14 has since been demolished. From Mountjoy Square east Father Conmee turns left onto Great Charles Street, where he passes the free church (now the Pavee Point Travellers' Centre) on the left. At the end of the street he turns right down the North Circular Road and Portland Row, passing North Richmond Street on the far side with its Christian Brothers school (13 North Richmond Street, another former Joyce residence, was the setting for 'Araby' in *Dubliners*). On the right he passes St Joseph's Church; the convent 'for aged and virtuous females' attached to the church is now a branch of the Dublin Institute of Technology.

182   'Near Aldborough house Father Conmee thought of that spendthrift nobleman. And now it was an office or something.' Aldborough House, one of Ireland's last Palladian mansions, was built in 1793-6 in the style of William Chambers. It is now occupied by a department of An Post.

At the Five Lamps, a well-known landmark among Dublin illuminations, he turns left onto the North Strand Road, passing Gallagher's at No. 4. Grogan's at No. 16, Bergin's and Youkstetter's vanished suddenly one night in May 1941 when they were hit by a German bomb

9. Aldborough House. Lord Aldborough, 'that spendthrift nobleman', was imprisoned in Newgate Gaol for contempt of the House of Lords. The last of Dublin's great townhouses, this building became the Post Office Stores Department.

from an aeroplane which had gone very much astray. They have since been replaced by Corporation housing, as was H. J. O'Neill's funeral establishment across the road at No. 164.

(184)   *Wandering Rocks ii* takes place at the undertaker's soon
(185)   afterwards at 3.15. Constable 57C, who saluted Father Conmee, now approaches Corny Kelleher, an ex-policeman who maintains his links with the force (he comes in handy later in Nighttown when he persuades the policemen to leave Stephen alone). Some information is then exchanged.

Father Conmee crosses the Royal Canal at Newcomen Bridge beside Charleville Mall, and steps into an outward bound tram 'for he disliked to traverse on foot the dingy way past Mud Island'. Mud Island on the left-hand side of Annesley Bridge Road, according to Weston St John Joyce, 'was a locality of evil repute in former times ... inhabited by a gang of smugglers, highwaymen, and desperadoes of every description, and ruled by a hereditary robber chief rejoicing in the title of "King of Mud Island".' The tram journey to the Howth Road stop, a distance of about 1 km, cost one penny, rather less than the equivalent bus journey today.

183   There is a bus stop on the left shortly after Newcomen Bridge. From here follow Father Conmee's tram journey by bus (Nos. 24, 51 or 53), passing the 'ivy church' on the left just before the railway bridge. Crossing the Tolka river by Annesley Bridge, pass Fairview Park (still to be constructed in 1904) on the right. On the left, off Fairview Strand, is Windsor Avenue, where the Joyces lived at No. 29 (one of their several Fairview addresses). Father Conmee alights at the Howth Road stop just past the Malahide Road on the left, and within view of 15 Marino Crescent, home of Bram Stoker, the author of *Dracula*.

'The Malahide Road was quiet. It pleased Father Conmee, road and name.' Father Conmee walks up the Malahide Road on his way to the O'Brien Institute, an orphanage where he will arrange for Paddy Dignam's son to be admitted. While walking he thinks of 'his little

10. The O'Brien Institute. Father Conmee's destination is now the Dublin Fire Brigade Training Centre. On the right of the picture is the celebrated Marino Casino, now open to the public.

book *Old Times in the Barony*, a memoir of the Athlone
184 area which was published in 1895. The fields of the
Marino estate on his left (now built over) remind him
of earlier years in Co. Kildare, and he imagines himself
reading his office on the Clongowes' playing fields. This
prompts him to reach for his breviary.

> A flushed young man came from a gap of a hedge
> and after him came a young woman with wild
> nodding daisies in her hand. The young man raised
> his cap abruptly: the young woman abruptly bent and
> with slow care detached from her light skirt a clinging
> twig.
> Father Conmee blessed both gravely...

The young man, as we learn on page 339, is Lynch,
who turns up later in the maternity hospital.

On the left, just past Griffith Avenue, is the O'Brien
Institute, a large building set well back from the road.
The next turn to the left leads to the Marino Casino, a
gem of eighteenth-century architecture designed by Sir
William Chambers for Lord Charlemont in 1762,
recently restored and open to the public daily during the
summer and at weekends in the winter. It is worth a visit
before returning along the North Strand Road to Amiens
Street (Connolly) Station. The No. 24 bus goes all the
way from Malahide Road near the Casino.

The station is the starting point for Tour 4.

Tour 4
Circe, Eumaeus, (Ithaca),
Lotuseaters,
Wandering Rocks (xvii),
Oxen of the Sun

Circe, 11.20 p.m.

350   *(The Mabbot street entrance of nighttown, before which
stretches an uncobbled tramsiding set with skeleton tracks,
red and green will-o'-the-wisps and danger signals...)*

The longest of all the episodes in *Ulysses,* this section
is set in what was once the most notorious brothel quarter
in Europe. Known at one time as 'Monto', after
Montgomery Street, it was famous in its heyday for the
establishments run by Mrs Mack, Bella Cohen and May
Oblong. It declined in later years, and one night in 1925,
at the instigation of the Legion of Mary, it was thoroughly
raided by the Irish police. The Legion of Mary followed
in the wake of the Gardaí and took charge of the 'fallen
women', many of whom were only too ready to find more
respectable employment. Although most of the streets
have been subjected to rebuilding and renaming, this
remains one of Dublin's danger areas where street crime
is common, and it should be treated with caution.

Throughout this chapter the 'real' action is
confusingly mingled with hallucinations generated in
the minds of Bloom and Stephen. These hallucinations

Tour 4

0   100   200 Yards

represent the enchantments of the witch Circe in the original *Odyssey*, who caused Ulysses' crew to be turned into animals (a theme echoed here in the continual descriptions of humans with bestial attributes). We will thread our way through this labyrinth, distinguishing reality from hallucination.

351   Among the grotesque figures in Talbot Street loom Cissy Caffrey, whom we last saw on Sandymount Strand, and the two English soldiers Private Compton and Private Carr. Stephen Dedalus and Lynch now appear, having

352 taken the train from Westland Row to Amiens Street Station (now Connolly Station). They would have left the station by the side entrance beside the Loop Line

353 bridge and crossed into Talbot Street. As they proceed into Nighttown they pass 'a liver and white spaniel on the prowl'. The dog reappears constantly in the episode, as a different breed each time.

    Modern-day Talbot Street has had its pavements widened and the roadway at the entrance is kinked to slow down motor traffic. On the way in to the street is a plain but imposing monument to the victims of the terrorist bomb attacks of May 1974, many of whom died here.

354   '(...*On the farther side under the railway bridge Bloom appears, flushed, panting, cramming bread and chocolate into a sidepocket*...)' Bloom, who got on the same train as Stephen and Lynch, missed the station and had to return from the next stop at Killester (or possibly from a nearer halt at Clontarf Road). Now, arming himself with provisions, he follows in their tracks along the south side of Talbot Street, past Gillen's at No. 64, in and out of Rabaiotti's at No. 65, and into Olhausen's at No. 72 to buy a crubeen and a sheep's trotter. Olhausen's still has the same name and location, though the sign proclaims that it was established in 1935.

355   By Cormack's pub (now Mother Kelly's) on the corner

11. Amiens Street Station. Stephen and Lynch, and later Bloom, emerge from the suburban line station at the end of the Loop Line bridge and cross Amiens Street into Talbot Street, on the extreme left. Later on Bloom and Stephen approach down the near side of the street from beyond the bridge.

before the lane he stops to look at the glow of a distant fire, then crosses Talbot Street after nearly colliding with 356 two cyclists and a sandstrewer. He reaches O'Beirne's pub on the diagonally opposite corner at the bottom of Mabbot Street (which later became Corporation Street and was recently, in an act of civic revenge, renamed 357 James Joyce Street), and enters Nighttown. His hallucin- 358–9 ations begin with a vision of his father; his mother and 360 wife also appear. He returns to reality briefly when a 361–7 bawd seizes his sleeve, but then he has visions of Gerty MacDowell and Mrs Breen, who finally fades from his side.

(...Followed by the whining dog he walks on towards hellsgates. In an archway a standing woman, bent

forward, her feet apart, pisses cowily. Outside a shuttered pub a bunch of loiterers listen to a tale which their brokensnouted gaffer rasps out with raucous humour...)

Bloom's path passes Foley Street (formerly Mont-
368 gomery Street) and Purdon Street. Nearby the two red-
coats and a drunken navvy are arguing with a shebeen-
369 keeper. 'Wildgoose chase this. Disorderly houses. Lord
knows where they are gone. Drunks cover distance double
370 quick.' He abandons the crubeen and trotter to the hungry
371–86 dog and drifts into another hallucination in which he is
arrested, charged with a long list of crimes and con-
387 demned. When the vision ends he has taken the third
turn to the right into Railway Street (formerly Tyrone
Street and Mecklenburgh Street).

(...All recedes. Bloom plodges forward again through the sump. Kisses chirp amid the rifts of fog. A piano sounds. He stands before a lighted house, listening...).

He has reached Bella Cohen's house at No. 81/82, on
the left-hand side just before the convent, where a block
of Corporation flats now stands. Here he is accosted by
388 'Zoe Higgins, a young whore in a sapphire slip'. Stroking
him, she discovers in his pocket a potato which he keeps
389 as a good luck charm, and takes it from him. Again he
390–407 hallucinates, becoming a popular figure, a successful
national leader and a worker of miracles. Dissident voices
arise and he is denounced and publicly burned at the
408 stake. Zoe invites him inside and they enter the house,
409 passing through the hall and into the musicroom, where
410 they find Stephen and Lynch with two whores, Kitty and
Florry. Stephen, drunk and confused, is making philos-
411 ophical speeches towards Lynch's cap, but is interrupted
412 by the noise of a gramophone in a nearby house. More
413 phantom visions arise, involving the End of the World
414–5 ('a two-headed octopus in gillie's kilts, busby and tartan
filibegs'), Elijah, and Stephen's listeners from the library.

416   Zoe adjusts the whistling gasjet, and as Bloom observes
417–22 her he has another hallucination, involving his grand-
        father Lipoti Virag and an appearance by Henry Flower.

        Stephen meanwhile is still at the piano, and touches
        the keys. The others request a song but he declines. 'No
        voice. I am a most finished artist.' His mind briefly
        divides into 'The Siamese twins, Philip Drunk and Philip
        Sober'.

423   Philip Sober reminds him of all the drinking he has
        already done around town, in 'Mooney's *en ville*,
        Mooney's *sur mer*, the Moira, Larchet's, Holles street
        hospital, Burke's,' but Philip Drunk continues recklessly.
        Florry asks him if he is out of the priests' college at
        Maynooth, and Zoe tells of the priest who visited the
424–7   brothel recently. The conversation continues with
        hallucinatory interruptions from Virag, the Philips,
        Henry Flower, Ben Dollard and others.

428   *(A male form passes down the creaking staircase and is
        heard taking the waterproof and hat from the rack.
        Bloom starts forward involuntarily and, half closing the
        door as he passes, takes the chocolate from his pocket and
        offers it nervously to Zoe.)*

429   Bloom speculates that the man in the hall is Boylan
        but relaxes when he hears a 'male cough and tread …
        passing through the mist outside'.

430   Bella Cohen, the whoremistress, now enters the room.
431–43 Bloom, awed by her dominating appearance, plunges
        into a long and harrowing hallucination in which Bella
        becomes a man and he himself becomes a woman. He is
        mistreated, dressed up, humiliated, put to work in the
444   brothel and auctioned to the highest bidder. In the depths
        of his shame he is confronted by the nymph from the
445–9   *Photo Bits* print in his bedroom, who reproaches him
        with his secret lusts and masturbations. Through his
450   fantasies leak sounds from the real world as Kitty asks

Florry for a cushion. Reality comes closer when his back trouser button snaps, breaking the spell.

451   Suddenly restored to an awareness of his own virility,
452 Bloom gains confidence. The nymph flees, and a moment later he is able to return the stare of the awesome Mrs Cohen with composure and contempt. This is a turning
453 point for him. Bloom gains further ground by reclaiming his potato from Zoe, and Bella descends on the swaying Stephen for payment. Confused by drink, he hands her
454 a poundnote, a gold half sovereign and two crowns – a total of two pounds, or ten shillings too much since the rate is ten shillings a girl. Bloom insists on paying for
455 himself, and prevents Stephen being cheated.

BLOOM

(quietly lays a half sovereign on the table between Bella and Florry) So. Allow me. *(he takes up the poundnote)* Three times ten. We're square.

He returns the pound to Stephen, who drops a box of matches and is still witty enough to make a remark about
456 falling Lucifers. Bloom offers to take care of Stephen's money before he loses any more.

457   Zoe reads Stephen's and Bloom's palms, and sees in
458–9 Bloom's hand something which causes her to whisper and giggle with Florry and the others. Excluded from
460–2 the joke, he slips into fantasy, imagining Boylan's visit to Molly with himself as a compliant and ridiculous
463 cuckold. Stephen and Bloom gaze together into the mirror and Shakespeare's face appears, horned and
464 uttering incoherent quotations. The whores persuade
465 Stephen to 'give us some parleyvoo' and he delivers a recital in broken English promoting some of the seamier
466 entertainments of Paris. He tells them of his dream of the previous night – 'I flew. My foes beneath me' – and
467 in a fantasy he sees himself as a fox, running from the

hounds. The hunt turns into a horserace with Mr Deasy bringing up the rear.

468 '(*Private Carr, Private Compton and Cissy Caffrey pass beneath the windows, singing in discord.*)' On cue, Stephen is reminded of the definition of God which he gave Mr Deasy – 'Our friend noise in the street.' The song they are singing is 'My Girl's a Yorkshire Girl' and Zoe sets

469–71 the pianola going with the same tune. Stephen starts dancing with all the girls, surrounded by fantasy figures including the music and dancing masters Professor

472 Goodwin and Professor Maginni. The others form couples and he continues dancing wildly on his own, whirling giddily till the music ends and he stops dead.

473 A horrible vision now confronts him – his mother, rising through the floor, her body dead and rotting. Buck Mulligan, who earlier accused Stephen of killing his mother, appears in the background to reinforce her

474 reproaches. The others only see that Stephen has gone

475 white, and Florry goes to get him some water. Stephen refuses to let his spirit be broken, and lashes out in rage.

(...He lifts his ashplant high with both hands and smashes the chandelier. Time's livid final flame leaps and, in the following darkness, ruin of all space, shattered glass and toppling masonry).

476 He dashes from the house, and the others rush towards the halldoor. Bella seizes Bloom's coat-tail and demands

477 ten shillings for the broken lamp. 'There's not sixpence-worth of damage done,' retorts Bloom, throwing down

478 a shilling and hurrying to the door. On the doorstep the whores are pointing at a disturbance down the street, and a hackney car arrives outside bearing Corny Kelleher and 'two silent lechers'. Bloom hastens past them and turns left along the street, seeing in his imagination a great crowd rushing after him with hue and cry.

479 '(*At the corner of Beaver street beneath the scaffolding*

Bloom panting stops on the fringe of the noisy quarrelling knot...)' Stephen, it appears, has addressed or accosted Cissy Caffrey while the soldiers were relieving themselves,
480 and a row has developed. Private Compton is urging Private Carr to hit Stephen. (Carr, incidentally, derived his name from a British consular official in Zurich, Henry Carr, with whom Joyce had a particularly ludicrous dispute in 1917. The incident formed the basis for Tom Stoppard's play *Travesties*.)

481 Bloom tries to pull Stephen away, but without success. Stephen, still rebellious against any attempt to master him, especially by his arch-enemies the Church and the State, makes a rambling reference to killing 'the priest and the king'. Carr seizes on this as an insulting reference to King
482 Edward VII, who immediately materialises, wearing a
483 white jersey and sucking a red jujube. Bloom tries desperately to calm the soldiers and remove Stephen, but
484 the argument escalates, attended by the imaginary figure
485 of 'Old Gummy Granny' (a grotesque version of Kathleen Ni Houlihan), symbolising the Irish nationalist cause. All this is lacking now is the third of Stephen's would-be-
486 masters, the Church. 'How do I stand you? The hat trick! Where's the third person of the Blessed Trinity? Soggarth Aroon? The reverend Carrion Crow.' This body is duly
487–9 represented by Father Malachi O'Flynn and the Reverend Mr Hugh C. Haines Love, M.A. (Mulligan and Haines in disguise, it would seem) celebrating a black Mass.

490 Lynch, who has been watching with Kitty, sneaks off,
491 and while Bloom still tries to calm things down, Private Carr rushes forward, strikes Stephen and knocks him out. The lurking dog, now identified as a retriever, barks furiously, and two policemen turn up. Private Compton
492 pulls Carr away, and Bloom is trying to explain matters to the police when Corny Kelleher appears. Knowing
493 Kelleher's influence with the police, Bloom enlists his
494 help in getting them to disperse the crowd and leave

495 Stephen alone. The policemen leave, followed by Kelleher
496 on his outside car, and Bloom stands by Stephen as he
497 gradually comes to. His last hallucination is of his dead
son Rudy. '...*a fairy boy of eleven, a changeling, kidnapped,
dressed in an Eton suit with glass shoes and a little bronze
helmet, holding a book in his hand.*'

Eumaeus, 12.40 a.m.

501   Preparatory to anything else Mr Bloom brushed off
the greater bulk of the shavings and handed Stephen the
hat and ashplant and bucked him up generally in
orthodox Samaritan fashion which he very badly needed.

The new chapter begins where *Circe* ended, at the
corner of Railway Street and Beaver Street. Fitting to the
condition of the protagonists, the style is weary and
clumsy, full of mixed metaphors, worn clichés and
stumbling syntax. The first priority is refreshment.

Accordingly [...] they both walked together along
Beaver street or, more properly, lane as far as the farrier's
and the distinctly fetid atmosphere of the livery stables
at the corner of Montgomery street where they made
tracks to the left from thence debouching into Amiens
street round by the corner of Dan Bergin's.

Montgomery Street, now Foley Street, still retains its
cobbles, and the remnants of the stable buildings survive,
though adapted to a less malodorous use. Dan Bergin's
pub is now Lloyd's. Many of the establishments which
they pass can easily be identified. Mullett's and the North
Star Hotel still bear the same names, the Signal House
is now Cleary's and Amiens Street railway terminus is,
of course, Connolly Station.

502   They passed the main entrance of the Great Northern
railway station, [...] and passing the backdoor of the
morgue (a not very enticing locality, not to say gruesome
to a degree, more especially at night) ultimately gained

12. The Custom House. After the fire of 1921, the Custom House was restored, but lost its chimney stacks and the statues over the portico. The wooden structure on the left is not, in fact, the cabman's shelter, which is just outside the picture.

the Dock Tavern and in due course turned into Store Street, famous for its C division police station.

The Dock Tavern, next door to the morgue, has now been redesigned and bears the name of The Squealing Pig, and the police are still in residence in a revamped 503 office nearby. Passing what is now the central bus station (one of Dublin's first public buildings in the modern style, designed in 1953 by Michael Scott), 'they made a beeline across the back of the Customhouse and passed under the Loop Line bridge'.

In one line Joyce mentions one of Dublin's most handsome constructions and one of its most abominable eyesores. The Custom House, designed by James Gandon and built 1781-91, appears at its most impressive from the far side of the river. Gutted by fire during the Troubles in 1921, the building has since been painstakingly and beautifully restored, with the replacement of much of the stonework. The Loop Line bridge was built in 1891 to connect the stations in Westland Row and Amiens Street and is constantly denounced for its impact on the view of the Custom House. The 'beeline' made by our two heroes across Beresford Place, rather dubious from the first, is now a suicidal impossibility due to the convergence of traffic from several different directions, and a patient use of pedestrian lights is advised.

504   Under the bridge, where Eamonn O'Doherty's statue of James Connolly now stands facing the site of his headquarters at Liberty Hall, Stephen is hailed by an acquaintance, 'Lord' John Corley (who appears in *Dubliners* as Lenehan's companion in 'Two Gallants'). Corley is down on his luck and asks Stephen to lend him some money. Stephen, who despite Bloom's concern did not hand over all his money to his care, discovers that
505 he has some halfcrowns in his pocket which he mistakes for pennies (the coins were similar in size though not in metal).

506   Bloom continues on his way with Stephen, attempting
507 to give him some advice about his choice of friends, especially after the scene at Westland Row Station where Mulligan and Haines apparently made it obvious that they did not want Stephen to come back to the Tower.

508   'Mr Bloom and Stephen entered the cabman's shelter, an unpretentious wooden structure…' The shelter stood under the railway bridge beside the south-west corner of the Custom House. Here Bloom orders coffee and a bun and they study the other occupants of the shelter,
509 including its keeper, who may or may not be the celebrated Invincible, Fitzharris, known as Skin-the-Goat.

In keeping with the original episode in the *Odyssey*, where Ulysses appears in disguise, there are continual references in this episode to mistaken and dubious identities, confused and disguised names and unreliable stories. It begins with the redbearded sailor who asks

Stephen's name and claims to know a Simon Dedalus
510 who turns out to be a circus sharpshooter. The sailor's
name is D. B. Murphy; by an appropriate chance this
appeared as W. B. Murphy until the Corrected Text
511 proposed a new identity for him. The picture postcard
512 which he produces is addressed, however, to Señor A.
513 Boudin. He is full of colourful tales, about the Chinese
514 with his little pills and the stabbing incident in Trieste,
515–16 but is elusive when questioned. Even the man's face
tattooed on his chest is capable of being changed.

517   Bloom is distracted from this entertaining spectacle
by the sight of a streetwalker looking in through the door
– the same one whom he saw earlier on Ormond Quay
and by whom he is scared of being recognised. He
converses with Stephen about the evils of prostitution
518 and then asks him 'as a good catholic' about his views
on the soul. Stephen's reply leaves Bloom a bit out of his
depth and he ventures instead to persuade Stephen to
519 tackle the coffee and bun. Their attention returns to the
520 sailor and his scarcely credible yarns, which are interr-
521–2 upted when the mariner goes outside to 'unfurl a reef'.
The men's urinal, to which he is directed and where the
others observed the Italians earlier, was probably at the
corner of the bridge with Eden Quay – too far for the
sailor to bother availing of it.

523–4   The conversation in the shelter turns to the subject
of Irish Home Rule and an argument begins between the
525 sailor and the keeper. Bloom takes up the subject with
Stephen and tells him about the incident in Barney
526 Kiernan's. Their views on nationality and nationalism
527 differ, and Stephen gets crosstempered, saying: '—We
can't change the country. Let us change the subject.'

528   Bloom picks up a nearby copy of 'the pink edition
extra sporting of the *Telegraph* tell a graphic lie' in which
he is momentarily jolted by misreading 'Hugh Boylan'
529 for H. du Boyes, and reads Hynes's report on the Dignam

funeral, which contains his own name, misspelt, and those of others who were not even there. Bloom is 'Nettled not a little by L. Boom (as it incorrectly stated) and the line of bitched type but tickled to death simultaneously by C. P. M'Coy and Stephen Dedalus B.A. who were conspicuous, needless to say, by their total absence (to say nothing of M'Intosh) ...' The paper also contains Mr Deasy's letter and an account of the Gold Cup race.

530   The others in the shelter begin a conversation about
531 Parnell, the possibility of his not being dead after all, and
532 Kitty O'Shea, who Bloom recalls had Spanish blood.
533 This prompts him to show Stephen a photograph of
534–5 Molly which Stephen politely admires. Bloom thinks it a pity that Stephen should be wasting his time with
536 'profligate women' and, further solicitous for his welfare, asks him 'At what o'clock did you dine?'

    —Some time yesterday, Stephen said.
    —Yesterday! exclaimed Bloom till he remembered it was already tomorrow Friday. Ah, you mean it's after twelve!
    —The day before yesterday, Stephen said, improving on himself.

537   Bloom decides to offer Stephen 'a cup of Epps's cocoa
538–9 and a shakedown for the night'. He pays the fourpenny bill and supports Stephen outside. Chatting about music, 'they made tracks arm in arm across Beresford place',
540 rounding the back of the Custom House inside the 'swingchains' at the edge of the road. Nearby a horse, dragging a sweeper, is being used to clean the street after
541 the horse traffic of the day. They stop as it crosses their path. Stephen, showing signs of recovery, is illustrating
542 the conversation by singing; Bloom admires Stephen's voice and considers advising him to concentrate seriously
543 on a singing career. They take advantage of a pause when

the horse stops to let fall 'three smoking globes of turds', and cross the wide roadway towards Gardiner Street Lower. The driver watches them as they disappear up the street in the direction of Bloom's house.

(*Ithaca*, 1 a.m.

The route from here to Bloom's house is described in Tour 3 and connects with it.) To continue this tour, cross Butt Bridge and turn left along George's Quay and City Quay, following the route presumably taken by Bloom between *Calypso* and *Lotuseaters*.

13. Eden Quay and Butt Bridge. The clock on the left belongs to 'Mooney's *sur mer*'. The centre section of Butt Bridge, in the middle of the picture, is mounted on a turntable.

Lotuseaters, 9.45 a.m.

58   By lorries along sir John Rogerson's quay Mr Bloom walked soberly, past Windmill lane, Leask's the linseed crusher, the postal telegraph office.

Bloom's unnecessarily circuitous route from home, taking him well down the quays, leads past Windmill Lane, now famous for its recording studios where Irish rock legends U2 made their way into history. A proliferation of tribute graffiti on the studio wall and surroundings led to the erection of a plaintive sign on the neighbouring building to announce 'This is not The Wall' and directing them next door to what is now clearly labelled 'The Wall'. Bloom passes Leask's, now the Columbia Bar and Grill, the post office next door and the sailors' home on the corner of Lime Street, where he turns right, away from the quayside. Brady's Cottages, on either side of Lime Street, are long since demolished, and the new apartment complex fails to match the squalid atmosphere conveyed by Joyce. He turns right along Hanover Street and into Townsend Street, which he crosses to turn left up Lombard Street. 'Bethel', the Salvation Army hall on the right, has gone, but Nichols' the undertaker still flourishes on the same side. Joyce House, home of the General Register Office opposite Nichols', is connected with the author of *Ulysses* only in name.

Crossing Great Brunswick Street (now Pearse Street), he goes up the right hand side of Westland Row and halts just beyond the railway bridge before the window of the Belfast and Oriental Tea Company (where the railings of the O'Reilly Institute now stand). Finally, holding a 59 *Freeman's Journal* which he has bought on the way from Eccles Street, he crosses to the post office, which was situated beneath the bridge approximately where the newsagent's is now, and collects a letter addressed to 'Henry Flower Esq'.

Strolling out of the post office and turning to the 60 right, he encounters M'Coy, and gazes idly past him during the conversation at the woman entering the carriage outside the Grosvenor Hotel, which stood next to the railway bridge across the street from the station. Conway's pub, to which M'Coy refers, is now Kennedy's 61 on the corner of Lincoln Place. Eluding M'Coy at last, 62 Bloom strolls on towards Brunswick Street.

>Wonder is he pimping after me?
>
>Mr Bloom stood at the corner, his eyes wandering over the multicoloured hoardings. Cantrell and Cochrane's Ginger Ale (Aromatic). Clery's Summer Sale. No, he's going on straight.

63 He turns right onto Brunswick Street, where the wall covered with hoardings has been replaced by a large student accommodation block (connected to the Trinity College campus by its own footbridge across Westland Row). The 'hazard' still serves as a taxi rank, but the cabhorses and the shelter are gone. 'He turned into Cumberland street and, going on some paces, halted in the lee of the station wall. No-one.'

64 Here in private he opens the letter. It is from Martha Clifford, whom he has never met and with whom he is

65 carrying on a clandestine erotic correspondence. He tears up the envelope under the railway arch, and reaches 'the open backdoor of All Hallows' on the right beyond the lane. This door, and the gateway to the side lane, are rarely left open nowadays, and it may be necessary to retrace the route back into Westland Row, past the station, and into the church by the front door to pick up Bloom's trail inside. Officially St Andrew's (by James Boulger, 1832-7), the church was also known locally as All Hallows, perhaps with some connection to the ancient monastery of that name which stood on the grounds now occupied by Trinity College.

66 Entering the church, Bloom finds communion in progress and takes a quiet seat in the corner, observing the proceed-

67 ings. The original of this episode in the *Odyssey* described the Lotuseaters, a hopelessly addicted band of dropouts; and

68 the so-called 'opiate of the people' becomes the subject of Bloom's thoughts here. He decides to leave before they come round with the plate, and emerges by the front door into Westland Row, next to the post office. Outside, he turns left.

'Sweny's in Lincoln place. Chemists rarely move.' The
69 'green and gold beaconjars' have gone, but Sweny's is still
there in Lincoln Place, at the far end of Westland Row,

14. St Andrew's Church. Called 'All Hallows' by Joyce, the church has changed little
since Bloom emerged and turned left towards Sweny's.

complete with its original name-plate, shop-front and
interior furnishings. Lemon soap is on sale there for the
many imitators of Bloom who call in. The real purpose of
his visit is to get some lotion made up for Molly; he arranges
to call back later in the day but eventually omits to do so.

70   Outside Sweny's Bloom is accosted by Bantam Lyons,
who has probably spotted him from inside Conway's.
Lyons borrows Bloom's paper to look up the Ascot
runners, and Bloom gets impatient. He tells Lyons he
can keep the paper.

—I was just going to throw it away, Mr Bloom said.
    Bantam Lyons raised his eyes suddenly and leered
weakly.

—What's that? his sharp voice said.

—I say you can keep it, Mr Bloom answered. I was going to throw it away that moment.

Bantam Lyons doubted an instant, leering: then thrust the outspread sheets back on Mr Bloom's arm.

—I'll risk it, he said. Here, thanks.

Bloom thus unwittingly gives a tip for the eventual winner of the Gold Cup, Throwaway.

Turning left, he walks 'cheerfully towards the mosque of the baths'. The Lincoln Place Baths, on the site now occupied by the Lincoln House building, were designed in Oriental style by Richard Barter in 1859. However, this establishment, which had closed in 1899, was not the one where Bloom goes for his bath. We discover elsewhere in the book that he went further on to the Turkish and Warm Baths, 11 Leinster Street. On the other side of Lincoln Place he observes Hornblower the college porter standing outside his lodge (an attractive stone structure which was taken down in 2001 to make way for another building) inside the back gate of Trinity College.

71   Continue along Lincoln Place into South Leinster Street. The last building on the right before the College railings was once Finn's Hotel, where Joyce's wife Nora Barnacle worked as a chambermaid. The name may still be seen in faded white paint on the gable wall, half-hidden by a tree. Nearly opposite Finn's an office block at No. 11 now occupies the site of the baths where Bloom foresees himself.

> He saw his trunk and limbs rippripled over and sustained, buoyed lightly upward, lemonyellow: his navel, bud of flesh: and saw the dark tangled curls of his bush floating, floating hair of the stream around the limp father of thousands, a languid floating flower.

After his bath, Bloom takes the tram to Sandymount for the funeral.

Wandering Rocks xvii

205   Almidano Artifoni walked past Holles Street, past Sewell's yard. Behind him Cashel Boyle O'Connor Fitzmaurice Tisdall Farrell, with stickumbrelladustcoat dangling, shunned the lamp before Mr Law Smith's house and crossing, walked along Merrion square. Distantly behind him a blind stripling tapped his way by the wall of College park.

Artifoni, having missed the tram outside Trinity, is walking to Ballsbridge. Farrell is on his way from the National Library, where he was signing the reader's book on p.177. On p.201 he was seen passing the Kildare Street club as he turned the corner into Nassau Street. The blind stripling, whom Bloom saw about two hours previously approaching Levenston's Dancing Academy in South Frederick Street, has since been up to the Ormond Hotel to tune the piano. Shortly after we see him here he will realise that he has left his tuningfork behind, and will go all the way back to retrieve it.

Farrell walks all the way to the corner of Holles Street, then turns and retraces his steps so that when the viceroy passes he is outside Finn's Hotel, staring at the head of Maurice Solomons in his optician's shop where he also served as the Austro-Hungarian viceconsul (p.208). The shop, at 19 Nassau Street, just beyond the Dawson Street corner, cannot in fact have been easily visible from here.

From Finn's Hotel (opposite the entrance to the Millennium Wing of the National Gallery of Ireland) walk along Clare Street and Merrion Square North, passing the landmarks of Farrell's walk in reverse order. 'Mr Bloom's dental windows' were at 2 Clare Street, where Marcus Bloom had his practice, and Law Smith's house was on the next corner. Between them at No. 6 were the offices of Beckett and Medcalf, where Samuel Beckett lived in the 1930s above the family firm and wrote his early novels. Across the next street, on the corner of

Merrion Square, was the former residence of Sir William Wilde and the childhood home of his famous son Oscar (who is commemorated by an unusual statue inside the railings of the green opposite). It was outside this house that James Joyce had his first rendezvous with Nora Barnacle on 14 June 1904. She stood him up. Halting at this corner, Farrell frowns northwards at the notice on Merrion Hall (now the Davenport Hotel), and southwards at 'the distant pleasance of duke's lawn' outside Leinster House (just beyond the National Gallery). 'Mr Lewis Werner's cheerful windows', on the corner house at the far end of Merrion Square North, are now preserved in the Kenny Gallery in Galway.

From here cross the street to the Maternity Hospital. The entrance is halfway down Holles Street, and a plaque there commemorates its connection with *Ulysses*.

Oxen of the Sun, 10 p.m.

314   Deshil Holles Eamus. Deshil Holles Eamus. Deshil Holles Eamus.

The National Maternity Hospital in Holles Street was opened in 1894, under the mastership of Dr Andrew Horne. Major rebuilding was carried out in 1934, including the neo-Georgian façade of the Nurses' Residence on the Merrion Square side. The Holles Street front was somewhat altered in style. Precisely in which room of the building most of the events take place is not specified.

The form of this episode was based by Joyce on the growth of the baby in the womb, from conception to birth. The language of the episode evolves historically as it goes along, beginning with primitive incantations, proceeding with what look like word for word translations from Greek and Latin and so through old and Middle English to a brilliant series of pastiches on the styles of the major writers in English literature, century by century.

315   After a short introduction dealing with fertility, childbirth, medicine and maternity care, Bloom makes his appearance. 'Some man that wayfaring was stood by housedoor at night's oncoming. Of Israel's folk was that

15. Holles Street Hospital in the early years of the century. Bloom enters by the 'housedoor' below the sign.

man that on earth wandering far had fared.' Bloom has arrived by tram from Sandymount, and has come to visit his friend Mrs Purefoy.

316   Lightning flashes as the nurse at the door, crossing herself, lets him in. She is Nurse Callan, who rented out a flat in Holles Street to the Blooms during their hard times some years previously. Bloom learns from her of the death of a young medical friend, Doctor O'Hare. He asks after Mrs Purefoy and learns that her long labour is nearly over.

317   Just then a medical student named Dixon, who treated
Bloom for a bee sting on Whit Monday at the Mater
Misericordiae Hospital, appears and invites Bloom to
join his colleagues and himself for a drink inside. Bloom
is reluctantly persuaded to sit down and take his hat off,
though he takes care to drink little, unlike the rest of the
318   company. Besides Dixon and four other students he finds
Lenehan and Stephen Dedalus, who has been drinking
all afternoon, all awaiting the arrival of Buck Mulligan.

Oxen of the Sun parallels an episode in the Odyssey in
which Ulysses' crew kill and eat oxen sacred to Apollo.
The students, too, show little respect for the sacred cows
of medical ethics, and embark on a jocular discussion of
319   whether to save the mother or the child in a birth where
320   it is a case of one life or the other. Bloom is painfully
reminded of the death of his baby son Rudy.

Stephen meanwhile, merry with drink, fills all the
glasses and shows off some money which he claims to
have received 'for a song which he writ', though in fact
it appears to be the remains of the morning's pay from
Mr Deasy, depleted by thirteen shillings which would
seem to have been spent on drink for himself and others.
Ready to show that for him especially nothing is sacred,
he poses a theosophical conundrum to prove that whether
Mary conceived Jesus wittingly or unwittingly, there is
321   nothing special in her by herself to be venerated. Punch
Costello, one of the students, starts up a bawdy song but
is silenced first by Nurse Quigley and then by his colleagues.

322   Tales of Stephen's womanising are told, while he himself reflects on his treatment by Mulligan which symbol-
ises his treatment by Ireland as a whole: 'Remember,
Erin, [...] how thou settedst little by me and by my work
and broughtedst in a stranger to my gates [...] and hast
made me, thy lord, to be the slave of servants [...]. Why
hast thou done this abomination before me that thou

323 didst spurn me for a merchant of jalaps…?' Even as he jeers at the futility of any attempt to relate our life to any sort of immortality, the thunderstorm breaks over them. 'A black crack of noise in the street here, alack, bawled back. Loud on left Thor thundered: in anger awful the hammerhurler.'

Stephen, interpreting the 'noise in the street' as the voice of an angry God, is frightened, despite Bloom's assurance that it can all be explained scientifically. A 324 pastiche of *The Pilgrim's Progress* tells how Stephen and his fellows are less interested in godliness than in whoring, protected by 'a stout shield of oxengut and […] they might take no hurt neither from Offspring that was that wicked devil by virtue of this same shield which was named Killchild'. Condoms are another desecration of this building devoted to the bringing forth of children.

325 Outside, as rain pours down on Dublin, Buck Mulligan, on his way from George Moore's in Ely Place, meets Alec Bannon outside Justice Fitzgibbon's at 10 Merrion Square North and invites him to come with him 326 to the hospital. Meanwhile a discussion has begun about the foot-and-mouth disease (the slaughter of oxen again 327 being relevant here), from which arises the tale of the two bulls, a fable about the two churches in Ireland. The first is the Roman Catholic Church, which arrived in Ireland in 1170 when the English pope Adrian IV (Nicholas Breakspear or 'farmer Nicholas') gave his blessing to Henry II's conquest of Ireland with his papal 328 bull *Laudabiliter*. The second is the Church of England, founded with Henry VIII ('the Lord Harry') as its head.

329 Mulligan and Bannon now arrive, and Mulligan proposes his scheme to buy Lambay Island off the north Dublin 330 coast and set himself up as a stud farm. Bannon meanwhile accepts a drink from Crotthers, the Scottish student, 331 and displays to him a locket with a picture of his girlfriend (Milly Bloom, as it happens). The conversation once

again turns to condoms – 'But at this point a bell tinkling in the hall cut short a discourse which promised so bravely for the enrichment of our store of knowledge.'

332   Nurse Callan enters to inform Dixon that Mrs Purefoy's labour is over and that the baby is a boy. Punch Costello makes ribald remarks about the nurse as soon as her back is turned, but he is rebuked by Dixon, who goes to attend
333–4 to his duties. Mr Bloom rejoices at the news but the others are less respectful in their comments. They burst forth in
335   a discussion of every type of abnormal birth from the commonplace Caesarean section to monstrous and deform-
336   ed births. Mulligan then conjures up for them a ludicrous vision of Haines, who, it seems, made a brief appearance at the soirée in Ely Place, witnessed by Moore ('the
337   dissipated host') and Russell ('the seer'), to tell Mulligan 'Meet me at Westland Row Station at ten past eleven'.

338   Bloom meanwhile is in a daydream about his youth, and then appears to nod off into a strange dream about a moving herd of beasts, about his daughter Milly and a mysterious writing which transforms itself into 'Alpha, a ruby and triangled sign upon the forehead of Taurus'.

339   Around him the others are discussing old times in Clongowes, the horse race, and Lynch's encounter with
340   Father Conmee that afternoon. Lenehan, reaching for a bottle of Bass, is restrained by Mulligan, who indicates Bloom's dreamy gaze fixed on the red triangle on the
341   label. Bloom comes to and pours Lenehan some ale. The conversation continues and they discuss such matters as
342   the future determination of sex and, to a greater length, infant mortality.

343   'Meanwhile the skill and patience of the physician
344   had brought about a happy *accouchement*.' The birth is over and Bloom is observing Stephen, remembering the occasion when he met him as a child at Matt Dillon's.
345   Suddenly – 'Burke's! outflings my lord Stephen, giving the cry, and a tag and bobtail of all them after...'

The revellers burst out of the hospital and turn right,
346 heading for the pub at the bottom of the street. 'Jay, look
at the drunken minister coming out of the maternity
hospital!' remark the boys in Denzille Lane across the
street, deceived by Stephen's 'Latin quarter hat'. They
reach Burke's on the corner of Holles Street and Denzille
(now Fenian) Street at ten to eleven. (The pub has been
demolished and replaced by a flower shop). Stephen
orders the drinks – absinthe for himself, ginger cordial
for Bloom, and five pints of Bass's No. 1 Ale, two pints
347 of Guinness and two whiskeys among the others. Snatches
of conversation are heard: Dixon telling someone about
Bloom, Mulligan remarking that Stephen's telegram message of the morning was 'Cribbed out of Meredith'; and
Stephen, the known possessor of money, being encouraged by his comrades to pay the barman for the entire
round of drinks at a cost of 'Two bar and a wing' (two
shillings and sixpence). Someone, possibly Lenehan, sees
Bantam Lyons drowning his sorrows in the pub.

348   'You move a motion? Steve boy, you're going it some.
More bluggy drunkables?' Stephen buys another round
as closing time is called – absinthe all round, except for
Bloom, who has a glass of wine. Bannon overhears
Bloom's name and realises 'Photo's papli, by all that's
gorgeous'. Mulligan has slipped away to the station. The
mystery man in the mackintosh is noticed; apparently
he is known as Bartle the Bread and has seen better days.

349   As they leave the pub Stephen and Lynch slip off up
Holles Street and along Denzille Lane, trailed by Bloom,
and emerge from the lane by Merrion Hall with its notice
'Elijah is coming! Washed in the blood of the Lamb.' Long
known as a gospel hall, the building is now a hotel. From
Lincoln Place they proceed down Westland Row to the
station, on their way to 'the kips where shady Mary is'.

From Pearse Station you may take the train to
Sandymount for Tour 2 (a) or Sandycove for Tour 1.

Alternatively, from Holles Street return round the east, south and west sides of Merrion Square, passing the houses of Daniel O'Connell (No. 58), W. B. Yeats (No. 52 and 82), Sheridan Le Fanu (No. 70) and George Russell (AE) (No. 84), Leinster House, and the National Gallery of Ireland, which has portraits of Joyce by Sean O'Sullivan, Wyndham Lewis, Frank Budgen and Jacques-Emile Blanche.

Tour 5
Wandering Rocks (xv, ix, xvi, x, xiii, xi, xiv, viii), Sirens

Wandering Rocks xv

—The youngster will be all right, Martin Cunningham said, as they passed out of the Castleyard gate.

Before setting out on this tour, it is worth visiting Dublin Castle, one of the city's most historic buildings, originally constructed in the early thirteenth century. Parts of it, including the spectacular Chester Beatty Library and the State Apartments, are open to the public when not in use for state functions.

16. City Hall. Martin Cunningham, Mr Power and John Wyse Nolan come out of the Upper Castleyard gate, on the extreme right of the picture, and walk across Cork Hill, on the left, passing the councillors on the steps of City Hall.

Tour 5

Cunningham, Mr Power and John Wyse Nolan emerge from the upper Castleyard gate, uphill from City Hall, with the list of subscriptions collected for Paddy Dignam's family. They pass City Hall (another impressive public building) and walk down Cork Hill into Parliament Street, meeting Jimmy Henry on the way.

Passing the watchmaker's at 30 Parliament Street, they 203 turn the corner into Essex Gate and meet long John Fanning in the doorway of James Kavanagh's winerooms. Thoroughly revamped in recent years, the premises are now described as 'The Turk's Head Chop House'. The doorway, which formerly led to a stairway and an upstairs lounge, is now an emergency exit and the stairs have gone. As they all go in and upstairs John Wyse Nolan watches the viceregal cavalcade riding past up Parliament Street. In interpolations we see the barmaids looking out of the Ormond Hotel window, and Blazes Boylan meeting Bob Doran in Grafton Street.

From the Turk's Head, cross Parliament Street to Essex Street, entering the celebrated Temple Bar area of the city, of which there is a map on the wall to the right. Take the second turn to the right into the laneway which leads to Crampton Court, beside the Olympia Theatre. Built about 1740 by Philip Crampton, the little courtyard with its arched entrance still exists but the west and north sides have been rebuilt in recent years.

Wandering Rocks ix

191   Tom Rochford took the top disk from the pile he clasped against his claret waistcoat.

It is not clear whereabouts in the court this exchange takes place – possibly at the side entrance to Dan Lowry's Empire Musichall (now the Olympia Theatre), or in the billiard rooms at No. 16 in the opposite corner (since replaced). Tom Rochford is demonstrating to Lenehan, M'Coy and Nosey Flynn his invention for showing what turn is on – presumably in the musichall programme. Lenehan is to canvass Boylan's support for the device.

Lenehan, who was last seen heading for Mooney's with Stephen, is now bound for another drink in the Ormond Hotel. He and M'Coy leave Crampton Court by the exit into Dame Street, turning left past the theatre and left again down Sycamore Street, past the stage door. The rescue from the sewer which Lenehan describes was a real event, which did not in fact take place until 6th May 1905 and which is commemorated by a monument on the site in Hawkins Street next to Burgh Quay. Rochford was only one of several people who were involved, including Constable Sheahan who died in the rescue attempt. Lenehan and M'Coy emerge next to the east corner of the Dolphin Hotel (now occupied by Bad Bob's Bar; but the west end has been preserved, complete with its carved dolphin, as an office building). Just to their right is now the National Photographic Archive, a section of the National Library of Ireland, which was the source for most of the photographs in this book.

They turn right along Essex Street, pausing at the bottom of Eustace Street to check the time in 'Marcus Tertius Moses' sombre office' – now Bruno's less sombre restaurant – and O'Neill's pub (recently renamed Farrington's, after the character in the *Dubliners* story 'Counterparts' who slips out of Crosbie and Alleyne's office up the street in the middle of the day for a quick drink in O'Neill's). St Winifred's Well, outside the pub, was unknown to Dubliners of 1904 and only rediscovered recently.

17. Eustace Street. Marcus Tertius Moses' office is on the right, with the triangular pediment over the door. The pub on the corner, Mullally Bros., was O'Neill's in 1904.

The Temple Bar area, through which they are walking, has undergone a remarkable transformation since the early 1990s. A maze of narrow streets originally scheduled for demolition in an urban transport scheme, it bred a bohemian culture of arts centres, restaurants and second-hand shops. When the scheme was dropped the tenants stayed on to become the vital ingredient in a new revitalised cultural quarter. It is a strange mixture of genuinely historical streets and buildings, exciting new architecture, outdoor art, cultural centres and more than enough 'fashionable' pubs and restaurants.

192   In Temple Bar (the central street which has since given its name to the whole area) Lenehan calls into Lynam's betting shop (location unknown) to place his money on Sceptre. (The Gold Cup race, scheduled for 3 o'clock (GMT) had already been run by this stage, but bets were, apparently, still taken until the result was telegraphed through). Inside he meets Bantam Lyons about to back Throwaway on the strength of his 'tip' from Bloom, and (unfortunately for Lyons) talks him out of it. Lenehan and M'Coy walk on towards Merchant's Arch.

Detour: *Wandering Rocks xvi*

At Fownes Street turn right towards Dame Street, passing on the right Cecilia Street where James Joyce briefly studied in the Royal University Medical School. The building is now named Cecilia House. Directly opposite the top of Fownes Street at 33 Dame Street is the site of the DBC restaurant. The present façade dates from the late 1980s but the next-door building with its balconied first-floor windows gives some idea of the appearance of the original.

204   As they trod across the thick carpet Buck Mulligan whispered behind his Panama to Haines:
—Parnell's brother. There in the corner.

Mulligan, having parted from Stephen on the way from the library, meets Haines, who has bought Douglas Hyde's *Lovesongs of Connacht* in Gill's bookshop in

O'Connell Street (passed by the funeral cortège earlier in the morning).

'—We call it D.B.C. because they have damn bad cakes,' explains Mulligan. The letters actually stood for Dublin Bread Company, later Dublin Bakery Company. There were several of these DBC tearooms around the city; it was in this one that Boylan was introduced to Molly Bloom (who afterwards left her gloves in the ladies' lavatory). The window where they sat was a wide one, with a good view over the street. At the next table is John Howard Parnell, the city marshal and brother of the dead nationalist leader. Bloom saw him earlier opposite Trinity College, presumably on his way to the DBC. His unnamed opponent at the chessboard could well have been Joyce's friend J. F. Byrne ('Cranly'), who played chess here regularly with Parnell and devoted a section of his memoirs, *Silent Years*, to accounts of their matches. Byrne's college nickname was 'The White Bishop'.

205 Over scones and butter and cakes and *mélanges* (probably coffee with whipped cream) they discuss Stephen Dedalus and decide that he is a lost cause. A few minutes later (p.208) they watch the viceregal equipage going past. (The interpolations in this section feature the onelegged sailor, who has reached Nelson Street, and the crumpled piece of paper thrown into the river by Bloom on p.125, floating 'beyond new Wapping street past Benson's ferry', practically as far as the present East Link toll bridge.)

Return down Fownes Street to Temple Bar and Lenehan and M'Coy.

Wandering Rocks ix (continued)

'They went up the steps and under Merchants' arch. A darkbacked figure scanned books on the hawker's cart.' Merchant's Arch gives access leftwards from Temple Bar to the river, directly beside the Halfpenny Bridge. This picturesque little thoroughfare is still lined with pocket-sized shops, and it is outside one of these that Lenehan and M'Coy spot Bloom (see *WR* x below). While Lenehan tells the story of the Glencree Reformatory dinner they go through the arch, across to the riverwall and left along the river. Bloom will follow in their tracks (see Tour 5a below).

(Interpolations in *WR ix* describe Richie Goulding outside the Four Courts, the viceregal cavalcade emerging from the Lodge gates, Master Patrick Dignam leaving Mangan's in Wicklow Street, and Molly Bloom replacing the fallen card in 7 Eccles Street.)

Wandering Rocks x

193   Mr Bloom turned over idly pages of *The Awful Disclosures of Maria Monk*, then of Aristotle's *Masterpiece*.

Bloom, who left the library at the same time as Stephen, has travelled in the same direction – to the bookshops on the quays. Evidence suggests that he has already visited Clohissey's in Bedford Row, where Stephen browses a few minutes later. According to Hart and Knuth, Bloom is probably at Francis Fitzgerald's shop (now The Merchant Barber) on the corner of Merchant's Arch and Temple Bar. He selects for Molly a book named *Sweets of Sin* (which the scholars have yet to identify) and rents it from the
194   shopman, who appears from behind a dingy curtain strung across the back of the shop. '—*Sweets of Sin*, he said, tapping on it. That's a good one.' (Interpolations in this section refer to Denis J Maginni, who has made his elegant way all along O'Connell Street to the Bridge, and to the 'elderly female' leaving the Four Courts.)

To follow Bloom on his way to the Ormond Hotel, see Tour 5a below. Otherwise continue along Temple Bar and Fleet Street to the junction with Bedford Row.

Wandering Rocks xiii

198   Stephen Dedalus watched through the webbed window the lapidary's fingers prove a timedulled chain.

Stephen, having left Buck Mulligan near the library and Almidano Artifoni outside Trinity College, is now outside Russell's the jewellers at 57 Fleet Street. The discomfort which he feels would doubtless be increased by the discovery that the premises is now a popular pub named The Oliver St John Gogarty. A lengthy inscription on the wall around the corner reveals to the careful reader that Gogarty was 'Perhaps, the quintessential Irish

199 literarly figured' and the original of 'Buck Milligan'. He hears 'the whirr of flapping leathern bands and hum of dynamos from the powerhouse' next door, which recently relinquished its role to become a motor bike theme restaurant named The Thunder Road Café. Oppressed by the 'two roaring worlds' of time and space, he feels the urge to shatter them (as he does eventually, in Nighttown) but decides 'Not yet awhile.'

He turns and goes down Bedford Row. Clohissey's bookshop at Nos. 10-11 on the right has gone now, replaced by a garage entrance with large steel shutters. As he pores over an interesting book of 'Charms and invocations' he is interrupted by his sister Dilly, who has

200 crossed the river from Dillon's auctionrooms and has just bought a French primer with one of the precious pennies she coaxed out of her father. (It is of interest to note that a French-English dictionary bearing the name 'John Stanislaus Joyce' and the address '7 St Peter's Terrace, Cabra' is in the collection at the Joyce Tower.) Stephen gives his approval, and inwardly stifles the urge to help his family, knowing that he will only sink with them.

This is the last we see of Stephen for some time. From here he goes to spend his money on drink in the Moira Hotel in Trinity Street and Larchet's in College Green, five minutes' walk from Bedford Row. (The interpolations in this section describe the two women whom Stephen saw on Sandymount Strand, returning from their expedition with their cockles, and Father Conmee, now walking through Donnycarney.)

Follow Bedford Row down to the river and turn right along Aston Quay, then cross the river by O'Connell Bridge and turn left along Bachelor's Walk, passing the entrance to Williams's Row.

Wandering Rocks xi

195   The lacquey by the door of Dillon's auctionrooms shook his handbell twice again and viewed himself in the chalked mirror of the cabinet.

The auctionrooms where Dilly has been loitering for the past couple of hours are now occupied by the entrance to the Arlington Hotel.

'Mr Dedalus, tugging a long moustache, came round from Williams's row.' Mr Dedalus has presumably come up Williams's Row from the Oval pub in Abbey Street, where he was drinking with Ned Lambert and other cronies. The lane has since been named Bachelors Way, but a rusted and almost illegible sign remains to proclaim the original title. Because the lane is obscured from this angle, Dilly cannot tell which direction he came from and thinks he may have been further away in the Scotch House on Burgh Quay. Bloom would also have come this way earlier from the newspaper office when he went to talk to Alexander Keyes here in Dillon's.

196   Dilly persuades her father to hand over a shilling and two pennies, and he walks on along the quays towards the Ormond Hotel, while she crosses the river to the bookshop in Bedford Row. (In the interpolations we see the runners in the College races, Mr Kernan in James's Street, and the viceregal cavalcade leaving the Park.)

Continue with Mr Dedalus along the quays past the

metal bridge, known as the Halfpenny Bridge because when it was first erected a toll of one halfpenny was levied on those who used it. Beside the bridge is the shop of the Dublin Woollen Company, for whom Joyce worked as an agent when he was in Trieste; the fact is commemorated by a display window containing facsimiles of his receipts and other information. Outside the Liffey Street front is a bronze sculpture by Jakki McKenna of two women shoppers sitting on a bench, jocularly known as 'The Hags with the Bags'. At the next corner on the quay is Swift's Row.

Wandering Rocks xiv

200 —Hello, Simon, Father Cowley said. How are things?
—Hello, Bob, old man, Mr Dedalus answered, stopping.

They clasped hands loudly outside Reddy and Daughter's.

Reddy's antique shop on Ormond Quay lower was on the east side of Swift's Row, near where the Millennium Bridge for pedestrians now spans the river. Father Cowley 201 is waiting for Ben Dollard, whom they see approaching from the metal bridge on his way from the Bodega in Dame Street. Ben Dollard is to intercede for Cowley with long John Fanning, the subsheriff, to call off the bailiffs placed on his house by Reuben J. Dodd. However it turns out that Cowley's landlord, the Reverend Hugh C. Love (who is not far away at that moment) has already distrained for rent and has the prior claim. Cowley's address, 29 Windsor Avenue, was a former residence of the Joyces in Fairview.

They continue along the quay, past Grattan Bridge. Mr Dedalus visits the 'greenhouse' or public urinal on the riverside pavement just beyond the bridge, and the others go on to the subsheriff's office farther along

Ormond Quay Upper. The subsheriff is in fact across the river in Kavanagh's at this time. Shortly afterwards they all meet up again in the Ormond Hotel. (Interpolations here describe Cashel Boyle O'Connor Fitzmaurice Tisdall Farrell, passing the Kildare Street Club on the corner with Nassau Street, and the Reverend Hugh C. Love passing Kennedy's at the corner of Mary's Abbey and Capel Street.)

Tour 5a: Alternative route to the Ormond Hotel; *Sirens*, 3.40 p.m.

Bloom, leaving Merchant's Arch with *Sweets of Sin* in his pocket, follows in the wake of Lenehan and M'Coy along Wellington Quay. As the action of *Sirens* begins in the Ormond Hotel, we get glimpses of him approaching in the distance.

(212)   'Bloowho went by by Moulang's pipes bearing in his breast the sweets of sin, by Wine's antiques, in memory bearing sweets sinful words, by Carroll's dusky battered plate, for Raoul.' Wine's at No. 35 is now X Music; Moulang's (now Tag Records) was at No. 31 (Hart and Knuth explain this inversion as typical of the musical techniques used throughout the episode), followed by Carroll's at No. 29 (now Planet Web).

(213)   'Bloowhose dark eye read Aaron Figatner's name. Why do I always think Figather?' He passes Figatner's the jewellers at No. 26 Wellington Quay and Prosper Loré the milliner at No. 22. The religious statues in Bassi's at No 14 remind him of his unsuccessful attempts to inspect the goddesses in the National Museum, interrupted by

(214) Buck Mulligan. He continues past Cantwell's at No. 12 and more religious goods at Ceppi's (Nos. 8-9). In between at No. 11 was Roger Greene's the solicitor's office. Here, a few minutes earlier, Gerty MacDowell watched the viceroy passing by while Lenehan and M'Coy took

leave of each other on the bridge. Bloom decides to eat before seeing Nannetti about the paragraph for Keyes; he considers the Clarence Hotel which he is passing (now an upmarket establishment owned by rock group U2) and the Dolphin in the next street, but goes on.

(215) 'Yes, Mr Bloom crossed bridge of Yessex. To Martha I must write. Buy paper. Daly's.' Bloom crosses Grattan (formerly Essex) Bridge. At this point, where the Poddle originally met the Liffey, was the entrance to the 'Dubh Linn' (Black Pool) which was situated behind Dublin Castle and which gave its name to the ninth-century Viking settlement that was formed on the river bank nearby at Wood Quay, location of the controversial modern Civic Offices which were built on top of the archaeological site.

(216) In Daly's, the tobacconists on the corner of Capel Street and Ormond Quay Upper (now a branch of the Bank of Ireland), Bloom buys 'Two sheets cream vellum paper one reserve two envelopes' for his letter to Martha.

(217) Catching sight of Blazes Boylan passing in a jaunting car, he moves on an impulse to follow it and almost forgets to pay for the stationery. He tenders a sixpence and gets fourpence change.

(218) Boylan alights and enters the Ormond Hotel. Bloom, hovering outside, sees Father Cowley outside Fanning's office and meets Richie Goulding approaching from the direction of the Four Courts. They decide to eat together and go into the hotel.

To find out what has been happening there in the meantime, we return to the beginning of the chapter. 'Bronze by gold heard the hoofirons, steelyringing.'

210 Joyce said that he wrote this episode in the musical form of a *fuga per canonem*. Its technique represents in words a number of musical devices, and the episode begins with a sort of overture which previews the various themes

211 of the piece. The action proper starts on the next page

with the two barmaids looking 'over the crossblind of
the Ormond bar' at the passing cavalcade.

18. Grattan Bridge. Daly's, where Bloom buys notepaper, is on the corner at the
extreme right. The Ormond Hotel, with its entrance and windows painted white, is at 8
Ormond Quay Upper; the 'greenhouse' is outside it by the riverwall. Marks's shop is to
the left of the hotel on the next corner.

The hotel has changed considerably since the first
Bloomsday. In 1904, when it was run by Mrs Nora de
Massey, the façade of the building was of a type with the
surrounding houses. Considerable alterations, however,
were carried out after a fire in the 1930s, and successive
changes have taken place over the years to 1998, when
the name itself was changed to the Ormond Quay Hotel.
The entrance to the hotel is still in the same place. On
the right as you enter, the reception area occupies
approximately the same space as the original bar, with a
window onto the street, although the structure and décor
are modern. On the left, where the modern 'Sirens
Lounge' now beckons the traveller, was the diningroom
where Bloom and Goulding ate and where they could

hear the music in the bar through the open door. The back bar, behind the lounge, retains its original features.

212   As the clatter of the viceregal hoofs dies away the boots comes into the bar with a 'tray of chattering china',

213 and Miss Douce and Miss Kennedy drink their tea despite a fit of the giggles over the 'old fogey' in Boyd's the druggist's. (Boyd's was at 46 Mary Street, next door to Dublin's first cinema, the Volta, which was opened in 1909 with James Joyce himself as manager. Joyce returned to Trieste within weeks of the opening and the cinema had to be sold soon afterwards.)

214   'Into their bar strolled Mr Dedalus. Chips, picking chips off one of his rocky thumbnails.' Mr Dedalus appears not to have accompanied the others to the subsheriff's office, having found the hotel too tempting a lure to pass by. He has barely sat down with his whiskey and

215 water and filled his pipe when Lenehan comes in, looking for Boylan. He left a message with Boylan's secretary earlier that he would see him here at four, his purpose apparently being to interest him in Tom Rochford's invention. Lenehan passes on greetings to Mr Dedalus

216 from Stephen, with whom he was drinking earlier in 'Mooney's *en ville*' (Abbey Street) and 'Mooney's *sur mer*' (now the Horse and Tram on Eden Quay).

    (Lenehan's movements for the day are fairly well documented. He first appears in the newspaper office around 12.30, and then joins Stephen in the two Mooneys'. Afterwards he calls in to Boylan's office in D'Olier Street and then goes on up to Crampton Court to meet Tom Rochford. The stroll along Temple Bar with M'Coy fills in time before his rendezvous at the Ormond. From here he will go to find out the result of the race and then repair to Barney Kiernan's; later he meets up with Stephen and joins the others in Holles Street Hospital.)

    Bald Pat the waiter comes into the bar to get a drink

for a customer in the diningroom. Mr Dedalus, perhaps not too interested in hearing about his son, wanders into the saloon, a separate room probably situated at the back

217 of the bar, and fingers the piano. The instrument has just been retuned by the blind stripling who left his tuningfork behind. Mr Dedalus strikes 'its buzzing prongs'.

218   As he begins to play the piano, Blazes Boylan arrives in the bar and orders a sloe gin for himself and a glass of bitter for Lenehan. 'Wire in yet?' he asks, referring to the result of the horserace. Both of them have put their money on Sceptre.

219   Richie Goulding and Bloom arrive in the diningroom and choose a table near the door. In the bar, Lenehan persuades Miss Douce '*Sonnez la cloche!*' and she performs her party trick of twanging her garter: 'Smack. She set free sudden in rebound her nipped elastic garter smackwarm against her smackable a woman's warmhosed thigh.' This is another sound to add to the many musical noises in this episode – the cavalcade, the teacups, the piano, Boylan's creaking shoes and so on. The organ of the body which Joyce assigned to *Sirens* was the ear, and there is plenty to entertain it.

    Boylan, aware that he is already late for his four o'clock meeting with Molly, tosses back his drink (a quick sloe gin, it would appear) and makes for the door before Lenehan can raise the business of Tom Rochford's invention. Lenehan gulps his bitter and hurries after him. They

220 leave the hotel and a minute later Boylan sets off in the jaunting car, along the quays, up O'Connell Street and North Frederick Street, along Dorset Street and into Eccles Street. The jingling of the car will soon be echoed in the brass quoits of Molly's bed.

    As Lenehan disappears outside, Father Cowley and Ben Dollard come in from the subsheriff's office. They have, of course, missed Fanning, but Dollard assures Cowley that 'Alf Bergan will speak to the long fellow'.

As they join Mr Dedalus in the saloon, Richie Goulding and Bloom order Power's whiskey and a bottle of cider from Pat, who gets them from the bar. Miss Douce is at the window, watching Boylan leave and wondering why her 'cloche' sent him going so quickly.

221 The trio in the saloon, unaware of Bloom's proximity, are recalling the night when Ben Dollard went to Holles Street to borrow a pair of trousers from Bloom for a concert. The trousers, as Bloom himself recalls soon afterwards, were a revealing tight fit. Bloom orders liver and mashed potatoes and Goulding has steak and kidney

222 pie. As they eat Ben Dollard launches into song: '—*When love absorbs my ardent soul…*' and Miss Kennedy serves two gentlemen at the bar. George Lidwell 'suave solicitor' enters the bar and is told that his friends (Mr Dedalus

223 and company) are inside. Rather than join them, he stays in the bar to have a Guinness and to flirt with Miss Douce. Lidwell was a real-life person whom Joyce engaged as his solicitor during the dispute over *Dubliners* with George Roberts, and with whom he had at least one meeting here in the Ormond Hotel bar; he was, however, ineffectual in the case and actually took Roberts' side.

Dollard and Cowley try to persuade Mr Dedalus to

224 sing; but at first he only plays '—*All is lost now*' on the

225 piano, overheard by the diners. At length he sings, '—*When first I saw that form endearing*', and Bloom signals to Pat 'to set ajar the door of the bar' so that they can hear better. Listening, Bloom takes the elastic band off his packet of notepaper and winds it round his fingers.

226 The song, he realises, is from Flotow's *Martha*. '*Martha* it is. Coincidence. Just going to write. Lionel's song.'

227 Mr Dedalus finishes the song amid applause, and Tom Kernan turns up (we last saw him on page 207, vainly greeting the viceroy further along the quays at Bloody

228 Bridge). Half-listening to Richie Goulding, Bloom continues to fiddle with the elastic band until it snaps. He

decides to write his letter to Martha here rather than in the post office, and asks Pat for a pen and ink and a

229 blotter. Pretending to be answering an advertisement, he produces his newspaper. 'He held unfurled his *Freeman*. Can't see now. Remember write Greek ees. Bloom dipped, Bloo mur: dear sir. Dear Henry wrote: dear Mady.'

Joyce himself used Greek E's when writing to a lady called Martha; this was Marthe Fleischmann, for whom he had a brief infatuation in Zurich in 1918-9. His letters to her, produced after his death, were at first believed to be fakes because of the unusual E's, but Richard Ellmann, Joyce's biographer, was able to verify them by reference to this passage.

Quickly calculating, he works out that he can enclose

230 a postal order for two and six as a 'poor little pres'. Finishing the letter, he murmurs, for Goulding's benefit, a false address while writing the real one. 'Messrs Callan, Coleman and Co, limited' come, of course, straight off the top of the Deaths column. He will buy the postal order at 'the postoffice lower down' on his way to Green Street where he has arranged to meet Martin Cunningham and the others for a lift to Dignam's house in Sandymount.

231 Through the bardoor he can see Lydia Douce holding to Lidwell's ear a shell which she brought back from her visit to the seaside. Bob Cowley is back at the piano, play-

232 ing the minuet from *Don Giovanni*. Appropriately enough, at that moment Boylan, of whom we have been given periodic glimpses (as we were earlier of Bloom) during his journey through the city, arrives at 7 Eccles Street and raps on the doorknocker. No more is heard of him, but the rap is echoed by a 'Tap,' the sound of the blind stripling's cane, which is repeated over the next few pages as he returns towards the hotel to fetch his tuningfork.

Bloom prepares to leave and pays for his meal, but lingers when he hears Ben Dollard singing 'The Croppy

233 Boy'. The story of the song comes through, bit by bit –
how the croppy boy makes his confession to the priest
and asks for his blessing before he goes out to die for
Ireland, only to discover that the 'priest' is a yeoman
234 captain in disguise. Bloom watches Miss Douce listening
and thinks of the effect of music on people's thoughts
235 and how absorbed she looks. He then notices Lidwell
and wonders if the absorption is really for him. Certainly
the motions of her hand on the beerpull seem to indicate
something not merely musical in her mind.

Bloom takes his hat, abandons his newspaper and
goes out past Pat, glances at the barmaids through the
bardoor, and scares the 'eavesdropping boots' in the
236 hallway. As he leaves the song ends and the trio return
to the bar. Their conversation continues while Bloom,
feeling lonely, turns right outside the door and walks off
along Ormond Quay Upper. 'Wait. Postoffice near
Reuben J's one and eightpence too. Get shut of it. Dodge
round by Greek Street.'

237 The cider, and the burgundy from earlier in the day,
are creating their own music as he walks past Barry's at
No. 12 (now a post office replacing the old one at No
34), and he is wondering how and where he can exercise
238 his wind instrument when he sees 'A frowsy whore with
black straw sailor hat askew' and recognises her; he had
once approached her in a lane but had been scared off
when she said that she had seen him with Molly. To avoid
her he turns and looks in the window of Lionel Marks's
shop on the corner of Arran Street (now a café). As the
blind man arrives at the Ormond Hotel Bloom views a
print of Robert Emmet in the window with the famous
last words of his speech in the dock: 'When my country
takes her place among the nations of the earth, then and
not till then let my epitaph be written. I have done.' The
print is possibly a souvenir from the previous year's cele-
bration of the centenary of Emmet's rebellion.

239   Taking the opportunity as a passing tram drowns the
noise, he lets his gases take their course. 'Pprrpffrrppffff.'

At this point one may follow Bloom's route from here
to Barney Kiernan's, or take Tour 5b below to the location
of *Wandering Rocks viii*.

Bloom passes Arran Street and goes on to the post
office at 34 Ormond Quay Upper, below Reuben J.
Dodd's office in the same building, which stood near the
corner of Charles Street and was demolished in 1998.
From here he apparently takes another circuitous route
towards Barney Kiernan's. He turns right either beside
number 35 or at the next corner beside the Four Courts.
(This imposing building by James Gandon, completed
1786-1802, housed the original four courts; Chancery,
King's Bench, Exchequer and Common Pleas. In 1922
its occupation by anti-Treaty forces precipitated the
outbreak of the Irish Civil War. The building was shelled
and countless irreplaceable archives in the adjoining
Public Record Office were destroyed. The Courts were
restored and reopened in 1931.)

At the back of the Four Courts he crosses Chancery
Street (formerly Pill Lane) and is seen on the corner of
Greek Street by the narrator of *Cyclops*, 'with his cod's
eye counting up all the guts of the fish' (p.244). He
appears to have filled in some time hanging round the
back of the markets before heading for Barney Kiernan's,
perhaps by going up Greek Street, turning right along
Mary's Lane and taking the third turn to the left into
Little Green Street. This street crosses Little Britain Street,
where Barney Kiernan's pub stood near the opposite
corner on the right. The action of *Cyclops* is described in
Tour 8.

By returning along Little Green Street as far as Mary's
Abbey, you may connect with Tour 5b, which begins
back on Ormond Quay Upper.

Tour 5b: *Wandering Rocks viii*

From the site of Marks's shop walk up Arran Street and turn right into Mary's Abbey. On the left hand side is Meetinghouse Lane, a narrow laneway in which is situated the old chapterhouse of St Mary's Abbey. Recently refurbished by the Office of Public Works, the chapterhouse now contains an exhibition on the history of the Abbey. It is open to the public from mid-June to mid-September on Sundays and Wednesdays (10 a.m. to 5 p.m.).

189   Two pink faces turned in the flare of the tiny torch.
        —Who's that? Ned Lambert asked. Is that Crotty?

19. The chapterhouse of St Mary's Abbey as it would have appeared in the reverend Hugh C. Love's photograph after the seedbags had been cleared out of the way.

Ned Lambert, who has left the Oval pub after drinking with Mr Dedalus, is now showing a visitor around the chapterhouse, which is being used as a warehouse by his firm, Alexander and Co. J. J. O'Molloy, having failed to borrow any money from Myles Crawford (p.121), probably joined the drinkers in Mooney's before going in search of his next touch, Ned Lambert. He enquires in the office on Mary's Abbey and is directed to the chapterhouse (p.185), where he finds Lambert with the Reverend Hugh C. Love, Bob Cowley's landlord. 'Crotty' is probably another of Alexander's men.

'—Yes, sir, Ned Lambert said heartily. We are standing in the historic council chamber of Saint Mary's Abbey where silken Thomas proclaimed himself a rebel in 1534. This is the most historic spot in all Dublin.' All these details, and more, are available within. The room once lit only by Love's vesta now has the benefit of electricity. The chapterhouse, with its present floor seven feet above its ancient level, is all that remains of a flourishing Cistercian Abbey, whose stones were used in 1678 to build Essex Bridge. The 'pillars' mentioned are probably a detail misremembered by Joyce. Love, who is writing a history of the Fitzgerald (or 'Geraldine') family, is interested in 'Silken' Thomas Fitzgerald, whose short-lived rebellion ended in his execution. A later scion of the family, Desmond Fitzgerald, a minister in the Irish Free State government in 1922, offered to propose Joyce for the Nobel prize for literature, but Joyce advised him against it, saying it would probably cost him his portfolio.

(In interpolations we see John Howard Parnell in the DBC and Lynch's girlfriend in Marino.)

190   Ned Lambert shows his visitor out, and follows with J. J. O'Molloy into Mary's Abbey. The clergyman turns left into Mary's Abbey and right into Capel Street towards City Hall (p.201), but then apparently turns left along Great Strand Street towards Cahill's corner on Liffey Street Lower and Lotts, where he is understandably 'unperceived' when the viceroy passes. The other two go round to the courthouse in Green Street, where J. J. O'Molloy does Lambert a favour in return for a loan.

Like most other earned or borrowed money in this book, it is promptly spent on drink, in Barney Kiernan's.

To follow their route, turn right into Mary's Abbey and right again along Little Green Street, which leads to Little Britain Street and to the courthouse just beyond it on the left hand side (see Tour 8). Alternatively, turn left and follow Abbey Street to O'Connell Street for Tour 6.

Tour 6
Aeolus, Laestrygonians, Scylla and Charybdis,
Wandering Rocks (vi, v, xviii)

Aeolus, 12 noon

96   Before Nelson's pillar trams slowed, shunted, changed trolley...

Halfway along O'Connell Street on the west side is the General Post Office with its imposing portico. Designed by Francis Johnston in 1815, shortly after the erection of Nelson's Pillar nearby, it was occupied in Easter 1916 by the Irish Volunteers and became their principal stronghold in the week-long rebellion which left most of the street in ruins. The GPO, gutted by fire, was later restored, and the site of the reading of the Proclamation of Independence by Patrick Pearse is marked inside the door. An extract from the Proclamation is displayed in the central window beside Oliver Sheppard's statue of the Irish hero Cuchulain, famous in literature for the unusual treatment given to it in Samuel Beckett's novel *Murphy* at the beginning of chapter four.

On the south side of the GPO is the cul-de-sac of Prince's Street. The area now occupied by Penney's department store was then the site of the ornate Metropole Hotel. Just behind Penney's, where the pavement angles into the street, was the entrance to the *Freeman's Journal* office. Prince's stores were farther along the street.

Tour 6

O'CONNELL STREET

Nelson's Pillar

G.P.O.

Mooney's
Newspaper Office
1, Lower Abbey Street

ABBEY ST.
Lemon's, 49 Lower O'Connell Street
Dillons

BACHELOR'S WALK

BURGH QY.

O'CONNELL
BRIDGE

WESTMORELAND ST.

Harrison's, 29 Westmoreland Street

COLLEGE ST.

Houses of Parliament
(Bank of Ireland)

Front Gate,
Trinity College

O'Donohoe's
(International Bar)
NASSAU STREET
TRINITY
COLLEGE
Mangan's
WICKLOW ST.
1-2 William Street

Adam Court
Brown Thomas

Davy Byrnes
GRAFTON ST.
National
Library

Thornton's
63, Grafton St.
DAWSON ST.
MOLESWORTH ST.
National
Museum

The Burton, 18 Duke Street
KILDARE

0   200 Yards

Appropriate to its location, the episode is set like a newspaper in short sections under headlines. 'Aeolus' in the *Odyssey* was the controller of the winds, and Joyce chose the lungs as the organ of the body for the episode. Accordingly there are many references to wind and breath. People rush in and out, doors blow open and papers whirl about.

Bloom, who has returned to the city centre with the funeral carriages, is inside the *Freeman* office, where Red

97 Murray cuts out a copy of the Alexander Keyes advertisement for him, and William Brayden, the owner, passes on the way to his office upstairs. Bloom takes the clipping through the building, 'along the warm dark stairs

98 and passage', into the *Evening Telegraph* office, which backed onto the *Freeman*.

20. O'Connell Street (formerly Sackville Street). Stephen and his companions cross the street past Sir John Gray's statue in the foreground. Before Nelson's Pillar trams, slow, shunt, change trolley and head in all directions.

Here he sees Hynes getting his account of the funeral in to the evening edition. It is taken by the foreman, Councillor Nannetti. Nannetti, an Italian Irishman, was indeed a councillor in real life and, as Bloom foresees, later became Lord Mayor of Dublin.

99 As Hynes passes, Bloom drops an unsuccessful hint about the three shillings which Hynes has owed him for the past three weeks. Bloom approaches Nannetti with

100 the ad, which requires a change in design, and offers to
run round and pick up a copy of the redesigned ad that
has already appeared in a Kilkenny paper. The foreman
101 agrees to give Keyes a three months' renewal, and Bloom
walks on through the caseroom towards the Abbey Street
102 exit. Passing the *Telegraph* editor's office, he goes in to
phone Keyes and finds Ned Lambert, Mr Dedalus and
Professor MacHugh laughing over Dan Dawson's speech
in the newspaper.

103   J. J. O'Molloy, a declining barrister, enters behind
Bloom. He has come to see Myles Crawford, the editor,
104 in hope of borrowing some money. Ned Lambert
continues to read the Dawson speech until Mr Dedalus
can take no more. '—O! Mr Dedalus cried, giving vent
to a hopeless groan. Shite and onions! That'll do, Ned.
Life is too short.'

    Myles Crawford appears from the inner office, where
he has been talking with Lenehan, the correspondent for
105 *Sport*. Ned Lambert and Mr Dedalus leave for a drink
in the Oval pub (just outside the office in Abbey Street)
and Bloom slips into Crawford's office to phone Keyes
106 as Lenehan joins the others. He is informed that Keyes
is in Dillon's auctionrooms in Bachelor's Walk, and goes
107 out to see him (probably via Williams's Row, now
Bachelors Way on the other side, which leads directly to
the quays). The others, at the window, watch in
amusement as the newsboys follow Bloom across the
street, imitating him.

108   Mr O'Madden Burke, tall in copious grey of
Donegal tweed, came in from the hallway. Stephen
Dedalus, behind him, uncovered as he entered.

Stephen's companion is not to be confused with O.
Madden, the rider of Sceptre, or Madden, the medical
student in Holles Street Hospital. Stephen himself, who
was last seen in Irishtown as the mourners went by, has

stopped on his way here to send a telegram from College
109 Green post office. Now he delivers Mr Deasy's letter to
Myles Crawford, who notices that a blank piece has been
torn off the end. Stephen recalls to himself the lines which
he wrote on the paper.

110 Lenehan, who seems determined to let the wind out
of any conversation when it gets too serious, finally mana-
ges to parade his riddle: 'What opera is like a railwayline?
111 ...*The Rose of Castile.*' Myles Crawford, surveying the
array of talents gathered in his office, encourages Stephen
to write him something. '...something with a bite in it.
Put us all into it, damn its soul. Father, Son and Holy
Ghost and Jakes M'Carthy.'

This was precisely the challenge which Joyce rose to in
his own books, particularly *Ulysses*. The headline above
this section, quoting Crawford's remark "YOU CAN DO
IT!", has an unusual distinction in that it is the only occurr-
ence in the entire book of conventional quotation marks,
which Joyce normally never used, preferring italics or an
opening dash. Presumably employed here to convey the
form that a newspaper headline would have used, the marks
only appeared for the first time in the Corrected Text.

112 Myles Crawford recalls a brilliant coup by the
journalist Ignatius Gallaher (who appears in 'A Little
Cloud' in *Dubliners*) when he reported on the Phoenix
Park murders on 6 May 1882 (not 'eightyone' as
remembered here), using an advertisement to provide
map references. The victims of this famous crime were
Lord Frederick Cavendish, the Under-Secretary for
Ireland, and Thomas Burke, also of the viceregal staff.
The attack was carried out by a nationalist group called
The Invincibles, and on the evidence of an informer
named James Carey, Joe Brady and the other assassins
were hanged. Fitzharris (known as 'Skin-the-Goat'),
driver of the getaway vehicle, got twenty years in prison
and was let out in time to appear in *Ulysses*.

113   In the middle of Crawford's story Bloom rings up from Dillon's to discuss the Keyes advertisement. The editor refuses to be interrupted and Professor MacHugh advises Bloom: 'Come across yourself.'

114   Meanwhile the conversation turns to the subject of
115 oratory. J. J. O'Molloy quotes a polished period from
116 the lips of a fellow barrister, Seymour Bushe, and Professor MacHugh answers with the lofty speech of John F. Taylor, which was delivered, not in the College
117 Historical Society in Trinity as stated, but in the Law Students' Debating Society of Ireland in the King's Inns in October 1901. Joyce selected this passage for the only recording he made from *Ulysses* – apparently because the acoustic recording was more suitable to a declamatory speech than to the quiet tones of interior monologue.

118   'I have money,' remembers Stephen, and he proposes that they adjourn for a drink. As they proceed towards the door, Myles Crawford goes back into the inner office for his keys, and J. J. O'Molloy follows him in, seeing his opportunity to ask for a loan.

119   The others emerge down the steps into Abbey Street and turn left. (The newspaper office was destroyed in 1916. The entrance was situated where the Abbey Street door of Eason's is now.) As the newsboys burst out behind them with the freshly printed racing special, Stephen starts telling his story 'The Parable of the Plums' about the two Dublin women going up Nelson's Pillar. The tale is full of actions which are ultimately cancelled out by equal and negative ones. The money, for instance, is saved up, only to be spent; the plums are bought 'to take off the thirst of the brawn'; and when the ladies get to the top they get giddy looking down and a crick in their necks looking up, so they end up doing neither.

120   Myles Crawford appears on the steps just as Bloom returns from Dillon's. Why Bloom should be as far along the street as the offices of the *Irish Catholic* (now occupied

by the *Irish Independent*) is not clear. Bloom breathlessly asks Myles Crawford if he will grant Keyes a free paragraph of editorial ('a little puff') in return for his renewal of the ad; but Crawford uncooperatively replies

121 '—He can kiss my royal Irish arse' and turns back to J. J. O'Molloy, whom he is also unable to oblige. (J. J. O'Molloy later gets money from Ned Lambert, but only in return for a favour.)

Leaving Bloom standing uncertainly in Abbey Street

122 (where we will return to him shortly), the pubgoers reach the corner, hearing the end of Stephen's story, and cross

123 O'Connell Street by way of 'sir John Gray's pavement island', where a statue commemorates the founder of the *Freeman's Journal* and inaugurator of the city waterworks. Here the professor peers aloft and to his left at Nelson on his Pillar, a doric column 134 feet high which was founded in 1808 to support a 13-foot statue by Thomas Kirk of 'the onehandled adulterer'. Despite numerous proposals for its removal, the Pillar survived until the night of 7-8 March 1966, when the top half was expertly blown off by persons unknown. Army engineers blew up the rest (and shattered numerous shop windows) two days later. For a while afterwards *two* heads of Nelson were on the market, but the real one is now on display in the Dublin Civic Museum. The Pillar stood at the intersection of O'Connell Street, Henry Street and Earl Street. Its site remained unoccupied until 2002, when at the time of writing the erection is imminent of a towering needle-like structure almost three times the height of the Pillar. Designed by Ian Richie and variously titled 'The Millennium Spire' or 'The Monument of Light', the object is already known throughout Dublin as 'The Spike'. To this the statue by Marjorie Fitzgibbon of Joyce himself, nearby in North Earl Street, will turn a Nelsonian blind eye. The statue of Anna Livia, Joyce's personification of the river Liffey, which reclined further

up the street amid jets of water (and whatever was added to it) throughout the 1990s, has been moved to a quayside site opposite the Guinness brewery.

Stephen and the others are bound for Mooney's pub, which was on the north side of Lower Abbey Street next to the O'Connell Street corner. The pub exterior survives, but a building society now operates within. Nearby at No. 5 was The Ship pub, where Mulligan and Haines were waiting vainly for Stephen to make his 12.30 rendezvous. Between Abbey Street and the National Library Stephen also visits 'Mooney's *sur mer*' on Eden Quay, travelling nearly on the same route as Bloom, to whom we shall now return.

Back outside the *Telegraph* office, Bloom turns right out of Middle Abbey Street and walks towards O'Connell Bridge.

O'Connell Bridge. Bloom buys Banbury cakes from the barrow in the foreground. Ahead of him, on the extreme right of the picture, the timeball on the Ballast Office shows that it is after one o'clock (and the shadows confirm it). On the far side of Westmoreland Street is Harrison's, to the left of the building with the two arched doorways.

Laestrygonians, 1.10 p.m.

124   Pineapple rock, lemon platt, butter scotch. A sugarsticky girl shovelling scoopfuls of creams for a christian brother.

This chapter contains one of the most minutely detailed itineraries of the book and for that reason is especially rewarding to follow, so much so that in 1988 Bloom's lunchtime route was marked by a series of fourteen pavement plaques graced with the appropriate text. *Laestrygonians* begins outside Graham Lemon's sweetshop, where the incomplete remains of a sign reading 'The Confectioner's Hall' still exist above the modern shopfront. This stretch, between Abbey Street and the river, is the only complete block in O'Connell Street to have survived the destruction of 1916 and 1922; ironically, it has suffered more from an outbreak of garish shopfronts and fast-food restaurants which have sprung up over the past thirty years.

Reading a throwaway which advertises the gospel meeting in Merrion Hall, he reaches the corner with Bachelor's Walk and glances to the right towards the auctionrooms where he met Keyes earlier, noticing that Dilly Dedalus is still outside.

125   'As he set foot on O'Connell bridge a puffball of smoke plumed up from the parapet.' The brewery barges, plying to and from the Guinness brewery, had hinged funnels which were let down when they passed under a low bridge, releasing the 'puffball'. Bloom stops by the parapet, looks down at the gulls and throws them the crumpled throwaway (which is seen floating seawards in 'Wandering Rocks'). From an applewoman's stall on the pavement he buys two Banbury cakes (made of pastry and currants) and throws them also to the birds.

126   Stifling an uneasy thought that Blazes Boylan might have a venereal infection, Bloom looks ahead to the Ballast

Office on the corner in front of him. Now Ballast House, it was taken down in 1979 and rebuilt with some alterations, including the moving of its famous clock from the east to the north side. This was the clock which, in *Stephen Hero*, Stephen told Cranly 'was capable of an epiphany'. The timeball was part of a mechanism on the roof involving a copper sphere that fell down a pole at 1 p.m. precisely. Dunsink time (estimated from the observatory near Phoenix Park where Sir Robert Ball was the Astronomer Royal) was 25 minutes behind Greenwich time, and was official Irish time until 1914.

127 As he crosses Aston Quay to the Ballast Office the five 'sandwichmen' march towards him from Westmoreland Street, advertising Hely's in Dame Street where Bloom used to work. They spend the day walking up and down between the far end of Grafton Street and, probably, the far end of O'Connell Street.

'He crossed Westmoreland street when apostrophe S had plodded by. Rover cycleshop.' Crossing the street nowadays is a much more complicated business than in 1904. Bloom did not have to contend with cars, pedestrian lights, traffic islands and curbside railings on his way across to the cycleshop (the site, part of a modern block, was until recently occupied by the Manchester United shop).

128 Thinking of the old times when he was in Hely's, Bloom walks along the curbstone.

—O, Mr Bloom, how do you do?
—O, how do you do, Mrs Breen?

129 He meets Mrs Breen, an old friend, outside Harrison's Restaurant, now a newer establishment under the same name. The pavement grating outside, where the street arab stood breathing the smell of the food he could not buy, has gone, but something of the Edwardian interior 130 remains at the back of the premises. Mrs Breen and her

husband are on their way to John Henry Menton's office in Bachelor's Walk to take an action over an anonymous postcard reading 'U.p: up'. The most that scholars have been able to make of this cryptic message is that Breen must have had some kind of urinary complaint. As Bloom learns that their friend Mrs Purefoy is in Holles Street hospital, 'A bony form strode along the curbstone from the river staring with a rapt gaze into the sunlight through a heavystringed glass.'

22. Westmoreland Street. Bloom crosses under 'Tommy Moore's roguish finger' on the right, opposite the former parliament house on the left.

131   Cashel Boyle O'Connor Fitzmaurice Tisdall Farrell, also known as 'Endymion', was a well-known Dublin eccentric whose condition was reportedly due to a plunge into a vat in Guinness's Brewery (which was, in fact, full of carbon dioxide rather than stout). One of his tricks was to let off an alarm clock outside the Ballast Office when the timeball fell, which may explain his presence

at this point. Farrell continues on his way towards the National Library, dodging outside all the lampposts. Parting from Mrs Breen, Bloom follows Farrell past the *Irish Times* office at No. 31 (now replaced by the EBS 132 office) and the crossing at Fleet Street.

'Luncheon interval. A sixpenny at Rowe's? Must look up that ad in the national library. An eightpenny in the Burton. Better. On my way.' (Rowe's would have involved a detour to George's Street.) Bloom passes Bolton's on the corner of Fleet Street and walks on towards College Street.

133   Before the huge high door of the Irish house of parliament a flock of pigeons flew. Their little frolic after meals. Who will we do it on? I pick the fellow in black.

The magnificent Houses of Parliament in College Green, designed in 1729 by Sir Edward Lovett Pearce and enlarged in 1785 by James Gandon, lost their occupation in 1800 when the Act of Union merged the Irish and British parliaments in Westminster, effectively ending the prosperous Georgian era in Ireland. The building now houses the Bank of Ireland, but the chamber of the House of Lords was preserved and may be seen on request.

Bloom passes the statue of the poet Thomas Moore with its 'roguish finger' and the nearby public toilet which gave rise to the joke about Moore's famous poem, 'The Meeting of the Waters'. In a less genial description in *A Portrait*, Joyce says of the statue 'sloth of the body and of the soul crept over it like unseen vermin', while Trinity College is a 'grey block...set heavily in the city's ignorance 134 like a dull stone set in a cumbrous ring'. For Bloom, the college has a 'surly front'. Founded in 1592 by Elizabeth I, Trinity has produced such distinguished graduates as Jonathan Swift, Oliver Goldsmith, Edmund Burke, Oscar Wilde and Samuel Beckett. Its elegant buildings include the Old Library, containing its most famous treasure, the Book of Kells, an intricately illuminated manuscript of the Gospels dating from the ninth century.

Wandering Rocks vi

(188)   —*Ma!* Almidano Artifoni said.

He gazed over Stephen's shoulder at Goldsmith's knobby poll...

Here at the front gate of Trinity, Stephen, on his way from the National Library to Bedford Row, meets Almidano Artifoni, the professor of singing. (The

23. College Green. The tram in the foreground, with its conductor on the front platform, is travelling in the opposite direction to the one which Almidano Artifoni has just missed. Behind it is raised 'the stern stone hand of Grattan', and further back beyond the cabrank is King Billy's statue.

character is based on Joyce's teacher Benedetto Palmieri, and the name is taken from the director of the Berlitz School in Trieste.) Artifoni is, apparently, advising Stephen against abandoning his singing career. He had ideas like Stephen's when he was young, he says, he too thought the world was a beast. He feels that Stephen is sacrificing himself. A bloodless sacrifice, Stephen claims. Artifoni begs him to consider his advice, and Stephen promises to do so. Spotting the Dalkey tram, Artifoni takes hasty leave and trots in vain after it. He is obliged to walk to Ballsbridge, and arrives there just as the viceroy does. Opposite the gate, 'The stern stone hand of Grattan' is raised aloft on the statue of the greatest member of the old Irish Parliament.

135 Bloom approaches the Provost's house on the left, built in 1760 and still lived in by the Provost of Trinity. A former incumbent of the office was Dean Salmon, whom Bloom remembers here. On the other side of the street he sees John Howard Parnell, the city marshal, with his 'Poached eyes on ghost', passing Walter Sexton's (now Thomas Cook's Travel) on his way towards the DBC in Dame Street for coffee and chess. George Russell, the poet (better known as AE) and a young woman pass Bloom on the curbstone; Russell, like Farrell, is on his way to the National Library, probably after a lunch in the vegetarian restaurant in College Green which he was known to frequent.

136 'He crossed at Nassau street corner and stood before the window of Yeates and Son, pricing the fieldglasses.' The opticians on the corner moved some years ago and a new front was put on the premises by the ICS Building Society. Bloom looks up Grafton Street into the sun and holds up his hand to blot out the disk with his little finger.

137 He moves on past La Maison Claire, now a newsagent, and looks left into Adam Court, where he sees Bob Doran 'sloping into the Empire'. This is the back entrance of what is now Judge Roy Bean's bar restaurant on Nassau Street. The establishment's most famous phase began in 1926, when Jammet's Restaurant moved here from 27 Andrew Street (where in 1900 Jammet's purchased Corless's restaurant, the meeting-place of Chandler and Gallaher in 'A Little Cloud' in *Dubliners*). Jammet's became a favourite meeting-place of writers and artists and its closure in 1967 was the end of an era.

24. Grafton Street. Bloom approaches up the right hand side of this fashionable thoroughfare, passing the entrance to Adam Court beneath the clock. On the left are Switzer's and the corner of Wicklow Street.

'Grafton street gay with housed awnings lured his senses.' Grafton Street, still one of the city's most fashionable shopping areas, is now pedestrianised and has been repaved in brick. In Joyce's day this street was paved, not with cobbles or setts, but with hexagonal wooden blocks which could be lifted out when repairs to pipes and other surfaces were necessary. Similar blocks can be seen inside Front Gate in Trinity. The wooden surface would have produced the 'hoofthuds lowringing' which Bloom hears.

138

Brown Thomas, the department store which Bloom passes on the left, moved across the street in the 1990s to take over the premises of its long-term rival Switzer's. Their own site was sold to Marks and Spencer and still looks quite like it did a century ago. Passing here, Bloom considers buying a pincushion for Molly for her birthday on 8 September (also the birthday, as Joyce was mischievously aware, of the Blessed Virgin Mary).

Frank Budgen wrote of meeting Joyce one day in Zurich and asking after the progress of *Ulysses*. Joyce said he had been working hard all day and had completed two sentences. The time was consumed, not in choosing the words, but in seeking 'the perfect order of words in the sentence'. The lines in question, which occur as the hungry Bloom, caught by the sight of silk petticoats, daydreams of seduction, are: 'Perfume of embraces all him assailed. With hungered flesh obscurely, he mutely craved to adore'.

The corner premises, formerly Combridge's the stationers, are now part of the Marks and Spencer complex. Bloom turns left here into Duke Street.

On the left hand side of the street is the Bailey Restaurant, where Parnell and his supporters used to meet in the smoking room upstairs. In Bloom's time it was the haunt of Arthur Griffith and *his* nationalist followers, whom Gogarty later joined there. In the 1950s and 1960s it became a favourite meeting-place of Dublin writers, and for nearly thirty years it was the home of the front door of 7 Eccles Street, saved when the house was demolished, and officially unveiled by Patrick Kavanagh on Bloomsday 1967 with the words 'I hereby declare this door shut'. The Bailey was rebuilt recently and the door moved on to the James Joyce Centre, close to its original home.

Bloom's destination is the Burton Restaurant, beyond Duke Lane on the opposite side of the street at No. 18. 'His heart astir he pushed in the door of the Burton restaurant. Stink gripped his trembling breath: pungent meatjuice, slush of greens. See the animals feed.' Repulsed, however, by the crowd of dirty eaters, 'He came out into clearer air and turned back towards Grafton street.'

140   Instead he enters Davy Byrne's 'moral pub', still flourishing at No. 21 but greatly altered inside. The nicely planed curving oak counter and the shelves full of tins

139

are gone, and the walls are decorated with elegant murals by Cecil Salkeld, in one of which Davy Byrne himself appears in his later years, bald and with a large white moustache. Gorgonzola cheese sandwiches and burgundy are popular on Bloomsday.

As Bloom orders his burgundy he is hailed by Nosey Flynn in his nook. His gaze wanders over the potted meat on the shelves, reminding him of the Plumtree's ad placed under the obituaries and prompting thoughts of cannibals. The Laestrygonians in the *Odyssey* were cannibals, and appropriately for this lunchtime episode full of food and eating the organ is the oesophagus.

141   He sits down with Flynn, who hears about the concert tour and asks 'Isn't Blazes Boylan mixed up in it?' Involuntarily Bloom glances up at the 'bilious clock'. There are still two hours to go before Boylan's meeting with Molly. (Joyce specified in his schema that this episode begins at about 1 p.m. If Bloom's observation 'Pub clock five minutes fast' is correct – and he checked his watch on entering the pub – he has taken at least three-quarters of an hour to walk from Abbey Street, a journey which should only take twenty minutes at most.)

142   Davy Byrne joins them from behind the bar on his way towards the window. Nosey Flynn is considering the runners in the Gold Cup, and appears already to have scanned the edition of *Sport* which emerged from the newspaper office on page 120 with Lenehan's tip for

143 Sceptre. Bloom briefly considers the dewdrop coming down Flynn's nose again, then returns to his lunch. About six o'clock, he thinks, Boylan will be gone and he can head for home. In the event he lingers out much later.

144   He thinks of 'All the odd things people pick up for food'. The sunshine and the taste on his palate bring back memories of the day in May 1888 when he proposed to Molly on Howth Head – the same scene which is in her mind at the end of the book. Studying 'the silent

veining' of the oak bar, he thinks of the shapely curves
of the classical statues in the museum. In contrast to
humans 'stuffing food in one hole and out behind', the
145 goddesses, he realises, are differently shaped. 'They have
no. Never looked. I'll look today. Keeper won't see. Bend
down let something drop. See if she.'

He rises and goes out to relieve himself in the yard at
the back (probably where the exit to Creation Arcade is
now). In his absence Nosey Flynn tells Davy Byrne that
146 Bloom is a freemason. Although everybody will admit
that 'Bloom has his good points' nobody seems to trust
him entirely or to claim him as a close friend. It is perhaps
significant that no one he meets is on first-name terms
with him.

Paddy Leonard and Bantam Lyons enter, followed by
Tom Rochford. As they talk about the Gold Cup race,
147 Bantam Lyons claims to have a hot tip and indicates Mr
Bloom on his way out as the man that gave it to him.
After their drink Tom Rochford and Nosey Flynn will
go up to Crampton Court to show Lenehan and M'Coy
the invention, while Bantam Lyons appears soon
afterwards in the bookie's in Temple Bar.

Mr Bloom meanwhile turns right towards Dawson
Street, avoiding the ravenous terrier choking up its cud
in Duke Lane. He passes the Burton and William Miller
the plumber's (where another Miller now sells medals),
considering ways of watching the progress of material
through the digestive tract and calculating how much he
will earn if he can get Nannetti to insert Keyes's ad with
148 the accompanying paragraph as requested. He passes
Gray's at No. 13 (not, in fact, on the corner; Joyce was
misled by Thom's Directory which listed it as the last
number in Duke Street, the corner shop being in Dawson
Street) and turns right into Dawson Street, passing
Connellan's proselytising bookshop where the Tea Time
Express is now.

'A blind stripling stood tapping the curbstone with his slender cane.' The street is clear save for the Prescott's van outside Drago's on the near corner of Molesworth Street. The driver, Bloom presumes, is in John Long's (where Graham O'Sullivan's is now), 'slaking his drouth'. He helps the blind man across the street and follows him
149 along the north side of Molesworth Street. The post office which he passes is gone now, but a pillar box of the period still stands outside.

The blind man turns left down Frederick Street towards the dancing academy at No. 35 on the right. Bloom, musing on whether it is possible to tell colour by touch, decides to experiment. 'Might be settling my braces' he thinks as he passes what is now the Jones Lang Wootton office. 'Walking by Doran's publichouse he slid his hand between his waistcoat and trousers, and, pulling aside his shirt gently, felt a slack fold of his belly. But I know it's whitey yellow. Want to try in the dark to see.'

Ahead of him he sees Sir Frederick Falkiner entering the freemason's hall, on the left with its pillared doorway.
150 Passing a placard for the Mirus bazaar, he reaches Kildare Street and is just about to bear to the left towards the library when he sees Blazes Boylan approaching up the street. 'Straw hat in sunlight. Tan shoes. Turned up trousers. It is. It is. His heart quopped softly. To the right. Museum. Goddesses. He swerved to the right.' Anxious to avoid Boylan, he makes 'with long windy steps' for the gate of the National Museum.

This building, as Bloom recalls, was built in 1890 to the design of Sir Thomas Deane, along with the matching library on the other side of the courtyard. Before 1925, when Leinster House became the home of the Irish parliament, it was possible to walk straight across between the museum and the library.

To conceal his disquiet Bloom pretends to be searching his pockets for something. The various contents of his pockets are unearthed – the Agendath Netaim leaflet, his handkerchief and newspaper, his potato good luck charm and finally the soap. Reaching the gate, he is 'Safe!'

Inside the entrance rotunda of the museum were the plaster casts of antique statues (since removed) which Bloom proceeds to examine, presumably using his subterfuge of dropping something behind the backside of Venus Kallipyge. Unfortunately, as we gather later, just before he can 'certify the presence or absence of posterior rectal orifice in the case of Hellenic female divinities' he is surprised by Buck Mulligan, who addresses a remark to him. After this expedition he crosses to the library.

Before following him it is worth visiting the museum, despite its lack of divinities. Its most impressive room is the Treasury, where some of the finest examples of Celtic art are on display, including the famous Ardagh and Derrynaflan chalices and the Tara Brooch.

Another curiosity nearby is Buswell's Bar on the corner, which, although it is not actually mentioned by Joyce, 'has been granted the James Joyce Pub Award for being an authentic Dublin pub' (according to the bronze plaque outside which quotes – inaccurately, alas – Bloom's thought 'Good puzzle would be cross Dublin without passing a pub'). While Joyce would probably be surprised, given the degradations experienced by so many of his characters on licensed premises, to find the word 'Joycean' used in praise of any pub, it is true that the pubs in his works are generally places where the service is courteous and the conversation is lively and convivial.

Continue to the National Library by the gate from Kildare Street and enter by the door beneath the portico. Among the many documents of Joycean interest in the library's collection are some of particular importance. These include Joyce's fair copy manuscript of *A Portrait of the Artist as a Young Man* and the first copy of the numbered first edition of *Ulysses*, both given by him to his patron Harriet Weaver; a large collection of his business papers saved by his friend and secretary Paul Léon during the occupation of Paris and placed in the Library under seal until 1992; and a recently revealed draft manuscript of the 'Circe' episode of *Ulysses*.

The action of *Scylla and Charybdis* takes place upstairs in the Reading Room, which is accessible to those with a reader's card. At the head of the stairway leading up from the entrance rotunda is a monument to T. W. Lyster, the Quaker librarian. To your right as you face the monument is the entrance to the reading room. Behind the counter inside the door is another door which leads to the office where *Scylla and Charybdis* is set.

Scylla and Charybdis, 2.15 p.m.

151   Urbane, to comfort them, the quaker librarian purred...

In the librarian's office are gathered William Lyster, Stephen Dedalus, John Eglinton and George Russell (AE). Stephen, who has had three whiskeys in two pubs since we saw him last in the newspaper office, has come to expound his theory on *Hamlet*. John Eglinton (a pen-name; his real name was W. K. Magee) was the editor of *Dana* magazine and a member of the library staff. It was he who met Joyce at the library on the morning after he left the Tower in September 1904. George Russell (who passed Bloom in Grafton Street on the way here) was a key figure in the Irish literary renaissance and a close associate of W. B. Yeats. As editor of the *Irish Homestead* (disrespectfully known as 'The Pigs' Paper') he was the first to publish stories from *Dubliners*. His pseudonym was originally intended to be 'AEON' but a printer's error determined the name by which he was to become known.

The discussion which is in progress becomes a conflict between Stephen's Aristotelian logic and the Platonist approach of the others. Stephen's approach to Shakespeare to a certain extent reflects the approach which Joyce has presented to his own readers, that of seeing his writing as a 'portrait of the artist', filled with the experience of his own life.

Lyster is only destined to hear the conversation in part. Almost immediately he is summoned away to the 152 reading room by a 'noiseless attendant'. His assistant, Richard Best, 'tall, young, mild, light', joins the group, 153 having just seen off Haines, who has gone to Gill's bookshop in O'Connell Street. Best in later years was asked to give an interview on this chapter. 'After all, you *are* a character in *Ulysses*,' said the interviewer. Best retorted that he was no character but a real person.

154 Best raises the subject of *Hamlet*, and Stephen launches into his theme. He sails a difficult course, as Ulysses did in the *Odyssey* when he took his ship between Scylla, the monster on a rock, and Charybdis, the whirlpool. Almost inevitably he sees himself between 'the devil and the deep sea'. Carefully he sets his scene with a description of the Globe Theatre. 'Local colour. Work in all you know. Make them accomplices.'

155 Shakespeare, it is known, played the part of the Ghost in *Hamlet*. Stephen claims that he wrote the part for himself because he too had been betrayed by his wife with his brother. Russell feels that 'This prying into the family life of a great man' is unnecessary, 'interesting only to the parish clerk'. Joyce scholars would think otherwise. Stephen thinks of the pound he owes Russell, most of which he spent on a whore in Bella Cohen's (the same one whom he goes to see later, only to learn that she is 156 married). Because the molecules of his body have renewed themselves since he borrowed the money, 'I am other I now. Other I got pound'. On the other hand, his memory

gives him continuity; he remains himself. 'A.E.I.O.U.',
he concludes.

Stephen argues that Shakespeare's wife, Ann
Hathaway, was of major importance to his work, though
the others feel that she was merely a mistake. '—Bosh!
Stephen said rudely. A man of genius makes no mistakes.
His errors are volitional and are the portals of discovery.'
This is a very useful remark with which to explain the
occasional discrepancies which appear in *Ulysses*.

Lyster returns to the room as Stephen reminds his
157 listeners that Ann Hathaway was older than Shakespeare
and seduced him in a cornfield. 'And my turn? When?'
he wonders secretly. Stephen, for all his self-confidence,
is a lonely young man and longing for love. When he
looks at the book of charms in Clohissey's later on, it is
the one for winning a woman's love that interests him.
He is ready for someone to come into his life as Nora
Barnacle did into Joyce's at this time.

Russell rises; he is 'due at the *Homestead*'. A meeting
of the Theosophical Society may prevent him attending
158 George Moore's soirée later on. Stephen listens as the
others talk about the evening and mention several of
Dublin's prominent writers who are invited. His own
name is conspicuously absent, though Mulligan has been
asked to bring Haines. Moore is proposed as the man to
write 'our national epic', a task which many would claim
fell eventually to Joyce. Hart and Knuth have pointed
out that Moore's soirées were usually held on Saturdays,
not Thursdays.

159   AE leaves, taking with him a copy of Mr Deasy's letter
for the *Homestead*, and the discussion is resumed. John
Eglinton rightly points out that we know next to nothing
160 about Shakespeare's life. The books by George Brandes,
Sidney Lee and Frank Harris which provide the sources
for Stephen's argument are based very largely on
supposition and very little on hard fact. Stephen is aware

of the claim that Sir Francis Bacon was really the author of Shakespeare's plays and that 'cypherjugglers' like Ignatius Donnelly, author of *The Great Cryptogram*, had worked out that the printed texts of Shakespeare's works were in a cypher telling the real story of Bacon's identity (he was, it seems, a son of Elizabeth I by a secret marriage to Robert Dudley). However, he sails by this particular whirlpool and sticks to his theory. The period of Shakespeare's great tragedies indicates a time of sorrow and turmoil; 'the shadow lifts' at the time of the birth of his first grandchild, which revives in him his feeling for love.

161   Stephen claims that Shakespeare lost 'belief in himself' when he was 'overborne' by Ann Hathaway. Something in him was killed and he became, in a way, a ghost.

162   '—Amen! was responded from the doorway.' Buck Mulligan, the last person Stephen wants among his aud-
163 ience, appears in the room. Best tells him that Haines just missed him and Mulligan explains that he came through the museum. Again the conversation veers off course into a discussion of Oscar Wilde's *The Portrait of Mr W. H.* which Best describes as 'the very essence of Wilde'. 'Tame essence of Wilde,' thinks Stephen, watching Best.

'You're darned witty. Three drams of usquebaugh you drank with Dan Deasy's ducats'. It is worth noting that from this episode onwards we never see Stephen entirely sober. Others, however, were not so lucky. Mulligan produces the telegram which Stephen sent him from
164 College Green and describes the terrible scene in the Ship when Haines and he were waiting with '… our tongues out a yard long like the drouthy clerics do be fainting for a pussful'.

Having parodied Synge, he goes on to tell Stephen that the playwright is 'out in pampooties' for revenge after an insult to his front door (31 Crosthwaite Park,

Dun Laoghaire, fifteen minutes' walk from the Tower).
Stephen recalls Synge's 'harsh gargoyle face' from their
meeting in Paris. Lyster is summoned again, this time to
attend to Mr Bloom, whom he conducts to consult the
165 *Kilkenny People* for Keyes's ad. Buck Mulligan recognises
Bloom and tells them what he saw him doing in the
museum.

John Eglinton and Best invite Stephen to continue.
Stephen explains that Shakespeare spent twenty years
166 living it up in London while Ann (left like Ulysses'
Penelope) stayed in Stratford. We hear nothing of her in
all that time save that 'she had to borrow forty shillings
167 from her father's shepherd'. Stephen claims that she had
cause and occasion for adultery. If Shakespeare had not
been wronged, he adds, why in his famous will did he
leave her none of his possessions but his secondbest bed?

168 Stephen reinforces his idea that Shakespeare wrote
from experience. A money-lender himself, he knew how
Shylock operated. 'All events brought grist to his mill.'
Current affairs and topical events provided the themes
and material for his plays.

'I think you're getting on very nicely. Just mix up a
mixture of theolologicophilological.' The theory, it seems,
is more of a clever game than a serious belief. Diverted
briefly by Eglinton's challenge to prove Shakespeare a
169 Jew, Stephen steers back to Ann Hathaway, 'laid out in
stark stiffness in that secondbest bed', and her return to
religion in her old age. Eglinton, however, still feels that
170 'Russell is right. What do we care for his wife or father?'
Stephen, considering briefly the alienation between
himself and his own father, describes a father as 'a
necessary evil'. Shakespeare's father was dead when
Hamlet was written; Shakespeare himself was a father,
171 no longer a son. His role in the play and in his life as
playwright was that of a father and begetter.

Mulligan seizes on one of Stephen's remarks and has

an idea. Lyster returns, and Stephen introduces Shakespeare's three brothers, of whom two, Edmund and

172 Richard, are named in his plays, both in the role of villain. Shakespeare uses his own name, Will or William, here

173 and there as well. '—You make good use of the name, John Eglinton allowed. Your own name is strange enough.'

Joyce chose the name 'Dedalus' for himself with care. In Greek mythology Dedalus was the 'fabulous artificer' who built the labyrinth in Crete and later made himself wings to escape from that country. The Dublin described in Joyce's books was his labyrinth, and he was destined to escape from it. Stephen, however, only has an abortive attempt to recall: 'Newhaven-Dieppe, steerage passenger. Paris and back.'

Lyster is called away again, this time for Father Dineen, the Irish scholar who is famous for his authoritative Irish-English dictionary, and Eglinton asks Stephen to continue his story of the brothers. Stephen thinks briefly of his own brother in the Apothecaries' Hall in Mary Street, on whom he sharpened his theories as he has since done on 'Cranly, Mulligan: now these',

174 and presses on, pointing out that '… the theme of the false or the usurping or the adulterous brother or all three in one is to Shakespeare, what the poor are not, always with him.'

He goes beyond this to claim that all Shakespeare's characters arise from different aspects of Shakespeare's mind. Their sins are his sins. 'His unremitting intellect is the hornmad Iago ceaselessly willing that the moor in

175 him shall suffer.' Shakespeare is a parable for all men, concludes Stephen.

Mulligan's idea comes to fruition and he begins to scribble on a slip of paper. Eglinton realises that Stephen's whole construction may be merely a *jeu d'esprit*.

—…You have brought us all this way to show us a French triangle. Do you believe your own theory?
—No, Stephen said promptly.

176 Eglinton feels that if this is the case Stephen need hardly expect *Dana* to pay him for the privilege of printing the theory. He is the only contributor who insists on payment. '—For a guinea, Stephen said, you can publish this interview.'

Mulligan draws him away from the Shakespeare fans (who remind Mulligan that he is invited to Moore's) with the hopeful suggestion 'Come, Kinch, the bards must 177 drink'. They leave the office and pass through the readers' room where Cashel Boyle O'Connor Fitzmaurice Tisdall Farrell is writing his name in the book. As they reach the turnstile at the door, Stephen thinks he sees a girl acquaintance in a 'blueribboned hat', but they pass on to the staircase with its 'curving balustrade' while Mulligan tells of the visit he and Haines made that morning to the Abbey Theatre. (By taking a train from Sandycove Station after their swim, they could have reached Tara Street or Amiens Street station soon after ten o'clock and stopped at the theatre on their way to the Ship in the same street. How long they spent in the pub is uncertain, but Haines must have left some time before Mulligan and visited Best in the library.) The Abbey Theatre was at that time still in the process of formation, with the movement of the Irish Literary Theatre society into new premises at the former Dublin Mechanics' Institute ('the plumbers' hall'), and the first opening night did not take place until 27 December 1904.

Stephen recalls a couple of points he should have made in his theory, but is swept on by Mulligan with his droll remarks and news about the literary people in the theatre. '—Longworth is awfully sick, he said, after what you wrote about that old hake Gregory. […] She gets

178   you a job on the paper and then you go and slate her drivel to Jaysus.' It is small wonder that Stephen is not invited to Moore's.

In 'the pillared Moorish hall' Mulligan reveals the subject of his scribblings, a so-called 'play for the mummers', and laughingly reminds Stephen of a recent incident when he was discovered lying drunk in the corridor of the Literary Theatre's previous venue, the Camden Hall. This was based on a real incident. The 'daughter of Erin' who stumbled over Joyce's sprawled body was a Miss Esposito. When he was ejected by the Fay brothers Joyce recovered somewhat and began beating on the door and shouting 'Open up, Fay, we know you've got women in there.'

179   As they reach the exit door someone passes between them. It is Bloom, making his way like Ulysses between these two obstacles. Mulligan greets him a second time and notices that Bloom has taken an interest in Stephen, which he jokingly interprets as lust. They walk out under the portico and through the gate into Kildare Street.

From here all three travel in the direction of College Green, either by the same route by which Bloom approached the museum, or via Kildare Street and Nassau Street. Somewhere on the way Stephen shakes off Buck Mulligan, who goes to meet Haines in the DBC while Stephen encounters Almidano Artifoni outside Trinity. Bloom heads for the bookshops off Temple Bar, followed a few minutes later by Stephen.

Turn right from the library gate and follow Kildare Street to Nassau Street. On the right hand corner is the former Kildare Street Club, now the office of the Alliance Française. The magnificent interior of this gentlemen's club (designed by Woodward and Deane, 1861) has, alas, been removed but the witty carvings by C. W. Harrison (often attributed to the O'Shea brothers) may be seen on the exterior.

Here you may turn right to join Tour 4 at Finn's Hotel, or left towards the Grafton Street area to trace the routes of two Wandering Rocks.

Tour 6a: *Wandering Rocks v*

187   The blond girl in Thornton's bedded the wicker basket with rustling fibre.

Blazes Boylan, whom Bloom saw in Kildare Street about an hour previously, is now in Grafton Street at Thornton's fruit and flower shop beside Tangier Lane (now Dunne's Stores), buying pears and peaches for Molly. At the bottom of the basket go the port and potted meat, which he has presumably bought elsewhere. Outside the shop the Hely's men plod 'towards their goal' at the corner of Stephen's Green, where on p.188 they turn round and retrace their steps behind the intended site for Wolfe Tone's statue. (A foundation stone was laid during the Tone centenary celebrations in 1898 for a statue by John Henry Foley similar to his O'Connell monument, but subscriptions failed to meet the target and the project was eventually abandoned. A more modern statue of Tone has since been erected on a different corner of the Green).

'—Can you send them by tram? Now?' he asks, while in an interpolation we see Bloom in Merchant's Arch. A messenger boy on a tram from the corner of Nassau Street would reach Dorset Street and Eccles Street in about ten minutes. Boylan tells the girl 'it's for an invalid' and asks to use the telephone. His call (on p.189) is to his secretary Miss Dunne, who informs him of his appointment with Lenehan in the Ormond. Boylan then walks along Grafton Street towards Trinity College. Outside La Maison Claire he meets Bob Doran coming out of the Empire (p.202) and is seen by Master Dignam (p.206). When the viceregal cavalcade passes on p.208 Boylan is outside the Provost's house. Soon afterwards – possibly near O'Connell Bridge – he takes a hackney car (number 324, driver Barton James) along the south quays and over Essex Bridge to the Ormond Hotel (Tour 5).

Tour 6b: *Wandering Rocks xviii*

206   Opposite Ruggy O'Donohoe's Master Patrick Aloysius Dignam, pawing the pound and a half of Mangan's (late Fehrenbach's) porksteaks he had been sent for, went along warm Wicklow street dawdling.

Master Dignam, who came out of Mangan's (now Munchies restaurant) on the corner of Exchequer Street and South William Street on p.192, is dawdling along the south side of Wicklow Street, opposite the International Bar, still with its fine interior and O'Donohoe's initials in mosaic on the doorstep. At No. 33, Madame Doyle's (now Morgan's women's clothes shop), he looks in at the poster for the Keogh-Bennett boxing match. On the opposite side of the street is the doorway of No. 15a Wicklow Street, where according to Bidwell and Heffer[4] the action of the *Dubliners* story 'Ivy Day in the Committee Room' is set in an upstairs room. On the same side of the street, the 'aka' bar opposite Brown Thomas stands on the site of the Wicklow Hotel, where young Stephen in *A Portrait* heard the sound *suck* in the washroom.

In Grafton Street he sees Blazes Boylan, with a flower in his mouth, listening to Bob Doran outside La Maison Claire. Reaching the tramline at Nassau Street, he sees 'No Sandymount tram' and follows Artifoni's example by walking along Nassau Street in the wake of Artifoni himself, Farrell, and the blind stripling. Farrell, returning on his tracks, passes Master Dignam but the fact is not recorded. Finally, the viceroy passes him in Merrion Square as he stands waiting to see the parade go by. His route home, by foot or tram, brings him via Haddington Road (Tour 2).

Tour 7
Wandering Rocks XIX –
The Viceregal Cavalcade

William Humble, earl of Dudley, and lady Dudley, accompanied by lieutenantcolonel Heseltine, drove out after luncheon from the viceregal lodge.

As with *Hades*, this long route is best followed by bicycle, or by car with occasional detours.

The viceregal lodge in Phoenix Park, where this tour begins, was originally built in 1751-4 to the design of Nathaniel Clements. Now known as Aras an Uachtárain, it is the residence of the President of Ireland and is occasionally open to the public. Some minor roads in Phoenix Park have been closed and it is best to take up the route at the Phoenix monument halfway along the main road.

25. Parkgate. 'Saluted by obsequious policemen', the viceregal cavalcade sets off across the city. To the left stands the Wellington Testimonial.

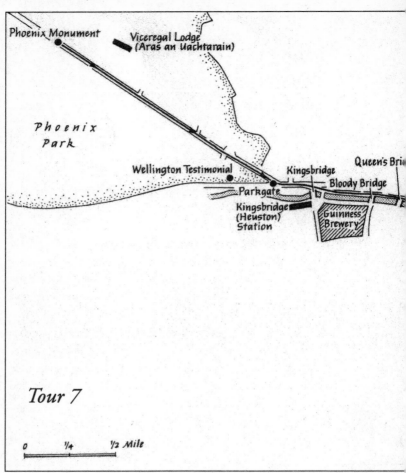

Tour 7

The park itself is the largest city park in Europe and one of the most beautiful. It derives its name from a spring of clear water (Irish *Fionn Uisce*) rising near the entrance to the present Zoological Gardens. Acquired by the Government in 1618, the grounds were first enclosed in 1660. The monument was erected in 1747 by the then Viceroy, Lord Chesterfield, who also laid out the grounds.

Drive from the monument towards Dublin. On the right hand side of the road, just before the next junction and opposite the Viceregal Lodge, is the site of the Phoenix Park murders. Also on the right, shortly before Parkgate, is the Wellington Testimonial, a 205-foot obelisk designed in 1817 by Sir William Smirke. This monument is prominent in *Finnegans Wake*, as are the Magazine Fort, also in this part of the park, and the Mullingar House Inn in Chapelizod, south of the park.

'The cavalcade passed out by the lower gate of Phoenix park saluted by obsequious policemen and proceeded past Kingsbridge along the northern quays.' The gates at the Parkgate entrance were removed, together with their piers, for the Eucharistic Congress in 1932. Two of the piers were re-erected more recently as part of a plan to restrict traffic through the Park.

The cavalcade follows Parkgate Street past Kingsbridge (leading to Heuston Station, formerly Kingsbridge Station, on the other side of the river) and proceeds along the northern quays. On the left is the Royal Barracks, subsequently Collins Barracks and now the Decorative Arts and History section of the National Museum of Ireland. On the opposite side of the river is the Guinness Brewery, followed by 'Bloody Bridge', a metal bridge erected in 1863 (see Tour 8). At the far side of the bridge is Tom Kernan, saluting 'vainly from afar'. Next comes Queen's Bridge. At the next corner on the left, outside the pawnshop at 32 Arran Quay, they pass Dudley White. After Whitworth Bridge the viceroy reaches the Four Courts, where Richie Goulding, emerging on his way to the Ormond, 'saw him with surprise'. Reuben J. Dodd's office, near the corner of Charles Street just after Richmond Bridge (the next block but one to the Four Courts) was above the post office (now demolished) at 34 Ormond Quay Upper; King's the printer's was on the west side of Charles Street at number 36. Opposite is Wood Quay, site of Dublin's oldest Viking settlement, where the Dublin Corporation offices now stand in front of Christ Church Cathedral. (The river Poddle, which 'hung out in fealty a tongue of liquid sewage', in fact emerges about halfway along Wellington Quay from an arched conduit in the river wall; it may be seen from Grattan Bridge.)

The viceroy passes the admiring barmaids in the Ormond, and Mr Dedalus on his way across the street from the urinal on the quay. (Hart and Knuth suspect that his hat is brought low to cover an open trouserfly.)

The reverend Hugh C. Love at Cahill's corner can neither
208 see nor be seen by the viceroy, who is watched by Lenehan
and M'Coy as the carriages turn right across Grattan
Bridge (also referred to in *Sirens* by its earlier name of
Essex Bridge). To the left on Wellington Quay, beside
Dollard House, is Gerty MacDowell, whose view of the
cavalcade is obscured by the vehicles stopped in front of
her. To the right, on the corner of Essex Quay, may be
seen Sunlight Chambers, formerly the offices of a soap
company, where a coloured frieze around the wall displays
the various stages in the manufacture and use of soap.
Straight ahead is City Hall, built in 1769 as the Royal
Exchange by Thomas Cooley.

26. The Four Courts. The viceroy surprises Richie Goulding here on his journey along
the north quays. Note the brewery barges on the river.

Beyond Lundy Foot's from the shaded door of
Kavanagh's winerooms John Wyse Nolan smiled with
unseen coldness towards the lord lieutenantgeneral
and general governor of Ireland.

John Wyse Nolan is at the back door of what is now
the Turk's Head Chop House in Essex Gate, on the right.

The viceroy goes straight on here, but motorists should turn left here into Essex Street (see detour below). Anderson's the watchmaker's was at No. 30 on the right, and Henry and James the tailor's shop was on the left at the corner with Dame Street. Also on the left still stands Read's the cutler's at No. 4, Dublin's oldest shop, which closed a few years ago.

Tom Rochford and Nosey Flynn, who have just come from Crampton Court nearby, are at the top of Parliament Street (site of Dame Gate in the old city walls) watching the viceroy approach. Here the cavalcade turns left (a privilege now reserved for buses and bicycles) and proceeds down Dame Street.

Detour for motorists: turn left from Parliament Street onto Essex Street, and take the first right turn up a narrow street beside the Dolphin. Turn left at the top to rejoin the viceregal route on Dame Street. (If the lane is blocked by an inconsiderately parked car you will have to drive on as far as Fownes Street.)

The viceroy and his equipage pass the poster of Marie Kendall outside the theatre, and the DBC tearooms at 33 Dame Street on the right. Directly opposite the DBC is Fownes Street, where 'Dilly Dedalus, straining her sight upwards from Chardenal's first French primer, saw sunshades spanned and wheelspokes spinning in the glare'.

Dilly has come by Temple Bar from her encounter with Stephen in Bedford Row. Stephen himself, who like Bloom does not appear on the viceroy's itinerary, is not far away, possibly even approaching up Anglesea Street on his way to the Moira Hotel in Trinity Street. This would make him, again like Bloom on Wellington Quay, visible to the viceroy but unmentioned.

Beside Fownes Street is the enormous Central Bank building, designed by Sam Stephenson and completed in 1978. This controversial building was already under construction when it was discovered that its height exceeded by thirty feet the limit laid down by the Corporation planning department, and it was obliged to live for several years without the copper roof which now covers the top of the building and the huge trusses from which the entire structure is suspended. The Bank is visible for a considerable distance over the Dame Street skyline.

Part of the Central Bank site was previously occupied by the handsome Commercial Buildings, in which was located the Bodega wine store where Ben Dollard had been with John Henry Menton (before walking down Crown Alley, through Merchant's Arch and across the metal bridge in *WR xiv*). Menton himself now stands 'filling the doorway of Commercial Buildings'. The façade of the building which faces onto the plaza is a replica of the Commercial Buildings front, at right angles to the original position. On the Dame Street front is a round stone plaque of a sailing vessel named *The Ouzel Galley*. The plaque, which was originally placed over the inside of the door where Menton stands, commemorated a ship which was posted missing at sea in 1695 and on which insurance was duly paid. Five years later it returned, having escaped, together with some considerable booty, from the hands of pirates. The Ouzel Galley Society, formed to settle the disposal of the treasure, remained until 1888 to settle other mercantile disputes, and from 1799 met here in the Commercial Buildings.

Next to the plaque, on the left at 11 College Green, was the site of Larchet's hotel and restaurant, where Stephen spent some of the afternoon and early evening drinking. Before this he was in Trinity Street (opposite, on the right) at the Moira Hotel beside Dame Lane, now rebuilt and occupied by Rio Coffee Co.

The Telecom Eireann offices on the corner of Anglesea Street are on the site of the old Jury's Hotel, which was demolished in the mid-1970s. Its Victorian bar, complete with fittings, was transported in its entirety to Pelikanstrasse in Zurich and reopened under the name of the 'James Joyce Pub'. The hotel is mentioned in *Ulysses*, one of about sixty licensed premises which share that distinction, but there is no indication that Joyce ever went in there.

The next block was formerly occupied by Daly's Club, of which the central section, designed in 1790 by Francis Johnston, survives. The Club was not only the most luxurious in Dublin but also reputed to be the most profligate. The rather more demure Kildare Street Club was founded as a polite alternative.

'Where the foreleg of King Billy's horse pawed the air Mrs Breen plucked her hastening husband back from under the hoofs of the outriders.' The Breens, who have failed to meet Menton in his office, are now on their way to Collis and Ward's at 31 Dame Street in search of a different solicitor. As we learn on page 246, Breen then meets Tom Rochford who sends him to long John Fanning; and from the subsheriff's office he continues up to Green Street courthouse. The equestrian statue of William III referred to here stood in College Green approximately on the site of the present statue of the poet Thomas Davis. The statue, which also features in a comic story in 'The Dead', was unveiled in 1701 and became the subject of repeated attacks. Frederick O'Dwyer notes in *Lost Dublin* that after a bomb explosion in 1836 which 'unseated' King Billy, 'Among the first on the scene was the Surgeon General, Sir Philip Crampton, summoned by a message that an important personage had fallen from his horse in front of the Bank of Ireland.' It was finally blown apart in 1928. The only piece that survives is part of the ornamental plinth by Grinling Gibbons, now on display in the Dublin Civic Museum. Opposite Trinity College the cavalcade turns right from Dame Street, a manoeuvre now forbidden to all vehicles.

27. Foster Place. In this picture, looking across College Green from beside the Bank of Ireland, may be seen King Billy on his horse.

Detour for motorists: continue left past the Bank of Ireland into Westmoreland Street (right hand traffic lane) and double back along D'Olier Street (centre lane) to College Street (left hand lane) and round past the front of Trinity College.

The procession passes the Hely's men outside Ponsonby's at 116 Grafton Street. On the left, opposite Pigott's at No. 112, Mr Denis J. Maginni, who attracted so much attention on O'Connell Bridge on page 194, is 'unobserved' by the viceroy. By the wall of the Provost's house on the corner of Nassau Street, Blazes Boylan 'offered to the three ladies the bold admiration of his eyes and the red flower between his lips'.

209 The cavalcade turns left along the railings of Trinity College, listening to the music played by the 'brazen highland laddies' in College Park, where the College races are under way. On the right, near the corner of Dawson Street, they pass Mr Solomons the optician in the Austro-Hungarian viceconsulate; on the left at the far end of the

railings, Cashel Boyle O'Connor Fitzmaurice Tisdall Farrell, returning from Merrion Square, stares across the carriages along the street at Mr Solomons' far-off head, aided by his 'fierce eyeglass'.

The carriages drive straight on into Clare Street without passing the back gate of Trinity in Lincoln Place where Hornblower the porter touches 'his tallyho cap'. Up until the 1980s the Trinity porters all wore hard riding hats with peaks. In Merrion Square they pass Master Dignam on his way home to Sandymount. Outside Holles Street hospital they pass the blind stripling opposite Broadbent's fruit shop (2 Lower Mount Street). Across their path goes the man in the brown macintosh, eating dry bread; he is next seen nearby in Burke's pub at closing time, where we hear that he is known as 'Bartle the Bread'. From Mount Street they cross the canal bridge (a famous 'Joycean slip' – it is the Grand Canal, not the Royal Canal) and drive on across Haddington Road (at the next traffic lights), where 'two sanded women halted themselves, an umbrella and a bag in which eleven cockles rolled to view with wonder the lord mayor and lady mayoress without his golden chain'.

The two women have come up from Sandymount Strand most probably by way of Bath Street, Church Avenue, Londonbridge Road, Bath Avenue and Haddington Road. Their observation gained an unusual complexity on Bloomsday 1982 when, in the re-enactment of *Wandering Rocks*, the parts of Lord and Lady Dudley were taken by the then Lord Mayor of Dublin (complete with golden chain) and the Lady Mayoress (to whom, romantically enough, he had got married the previous weekend).

The route leads straight on along Northumberland Road and past Lansdowne Road on the left. The house admired by Queen Victoria has not been identified, but Hart and Knuth have located at 14 Lansdowne Road the house of Benedetto Palmieri, part-original of Almidano Artifoni, who gives the final salute with his 'sturdy trousers swallowed by a closing door'.

It may be noted that, despite the assurance on page 207 that 'the viceroy was most cordially greeted on his way through the metropolis', he is in fact met with almost total indifference. The few 'cordial' greetings he does get either fail to be communicated or are given by mistake.

The viceroy continues towards Ballsbridge. To the right of his route is the circular American Embassy building, designed in 1964. His final destination is the Royal Dublin Society showground between Anglesea Road and Simmonscourt Road. The handsome buildings date from 1925, when the RDS moved their headquarters from Leinster House.

From the RDS you may drive on along the main road through Blackrock, Monkstown and Dun Laoghaire to Sandycove for Tour 1, or left down Serpentine Avenue to Tritonville Road to connect with Tour 2. Alternatively, you may leave Ballsbridge by Sandymount Avenue (passing W. B. Yeats's birthplace at No. 2 on the right) or by Shelbourne Road, where from March to August 1904 Joyce was living on the upper floor of No. 60, on the right.

King's Inns

(Site of) Linenhall Barracks

Barney Kiernan's

Courthouse

Richmond Hospital

Narrator talks with Insp.Troy

The Castle

Geraghty 29 Arbour Hill

Bluecoat School (Law Society)

15 Usher's Island

St Catherine's Church

Entrance to Guinness Brewery

Kingsbridge (Heuston) Station

Dr Steevens' Hospital

Swift's (St Patrick's) Hospital

Sundial

Crimmins (The Malt House)

Cromwell's Quarters

Royal Hospital

Bully's Acre

Kilmainham Gaol

Tour 8

BOLTON ST.

PARNELL STREET

MARY STREET

CAPEL ST.

ORMOND QUAY

PRUSSIA ST.   MANOR ST.   STONEYBATTER

BRUNSWICK ST.

KING STREET

SMITHFIELD

CHURCH STREET

BLACKHALL PL.

ARRAN QUAY

ELLIS QUAY

VICTORIA QUAY

THOMAS STREET

JAMES'S STREET

BOW LANE

MILITARY ROAD

MOUNT BROWN

KILMAINHAM LANE

0   100   200 Yards

Tour 8
Wandering Rocks (xii), Cyclops

A convenient point from which to start this tour is Heuston Station, beside the Liffey at Kingsbridge. It may be reached by the DART shuttle bus No. 90, which circulates around the quays between here, Connolly Station and Tara Street Station.

Before launching on the Joycean itinerary, it is worth visiting some of the notable buildings in the area. Just on the far side of the river is the former Collins Barracks, originally built as the Royal Barracks and continuously occupied by the military for nearly three hundred years until its recent acquisition by the National Museum of Ireland for the display of its collections. A visit here is an expedition in itself, however, and best left to another day. Also near at hand is the Royal Hospital in Kilmainham, which is within five minutes walk of the station on Military Road (to the left just beyond the station). The hospital, founded in 1680 by James Butler, first duke of Ormonde, 'for the reception and entertainment of ancient, maimed and infirm officers and soldiers,' is perhaps the oldest building in Dublin to retain its original structure. Restored and opened to the public in 1985, the former residential section is now the home of the Irish Museum of Modern Art, while the impressive Great Hall and Chapel are preserved for visits and functions. The Royal Hospital is open daily.

The avenue at the far side of the hospital building leads past an ancient graveyard known as Bully's Acre to a striking battlemented gate designed in 1812 by Francis Johnston, which originally stood on the quays at the foot of Watling Street but which was moved to its present location in 1846. Across the road on the far side of the gate is Kilmainham Gaol, built 1787-92 and finally closed in 1924. In its time it housed many celebrated inmates, including the Fenians in 1866, Parnell and his Land League associates in 1881, the Invincibles in 1883 and, in 1916, the Volunteers, several of whose leaders were shot here. With its classic prison interior it has often been used for films. In the exhibition area, informative displays and memorabilia of the gaol's many political prisoners trace the history of the struggle for Irish freedom, while in a separate section the penal system in general is harrowingly explored through a series of interactive exhibits. Kilmainham Gaol is open daily.

Follow the outside wall of the Royal Hospital either from Military Road or from Kilmainham Lane to Bow Bridge. Here a set of steps named Cromwell's Quarters (known previous to 1876 as Murdering Lane) leads to Mount Brown. Turn left here towards James's Street.

Shorter route: Heuston Station to James's Street

If not visiting Kilmainham, follow Steevens' Lane from opposite the station. On the right is Dr Steevens' Hospital, built in 1720 by Thomas Burgh on a bequest from Dr Richard Steevens. Grissel Steevens, the doctor's sister, whose name appears with his above the east door, had rooms in the hospital and was reputed, according to legend, to have the face of a pig. The building, with its fine quadrangle, housed the oldest public hospital in Ireland until its closure in 1987. It now houses the offices of the Eastern Health Board.

At the top of the lane on the right is St Patrick's Hospital, commonly known as Swift's Hospital after its founder, the celebrated author of *Gulliver's Travels*. Built by George Semple and opened in 1757, it is still a psychiatric hospital and contains some relics of Swift which may be viewed by arrangement.

Turn left into Bow Lane and immediately right into James's Street. Almost directly opposite, The Malt House at 27-28 James's Street was formerly Crimmins' pub, from which Tom Kernan has just emerged, glowing with gin and pleasure. A plaque on the pub commemorates its moment in literary history, and Crimmins' original nameboard can be seen displayed on the wall inside, to the left of the entrance. As this section begins, Mr Kernan has just reached the junction of James's Street with Bow Lane.

196   'From the sundial towards James's gate walked Mr Kernan, pleased with the order he had booked ...' The sundial on its tall pillar, erected around 1813 by the Dublin Paving Board, was handsomely restored in 1995 and made the central feature of a small paved park with seats beneath its trees.

On Mr Kernan's right were Shackleton's offices at No. 35 (now a vacant space between Crampton's and Steel Fixing Services). Mr Kernan is pleased with the way he has persuaded Crimmins (a tea, wine and spirit merchant) to take another order of tea – 'the cup that cheers but not inebriates' – from Pulbrook Robertson, for whom Kernan is an agent. His mind runs back over their conversation about the *General Slocum* disaster, an appalling incident, reported in the day's papers, involving a fire on a riverboat on New York's East River in which 1,021 people, out for the day on a Sunday School picnic, lost their lives.

197   Mr Kernan pauses to admire himself in 'the sloping mirror of Peter Kennedy, hairdresser' (now the Fish and Poultry shop). The frockcoat of which he is so proud did not attract the attention of Mr Bloom at the funeral that morning, although it is possible that he was not wearing

it then. As he looks across the road at someone who looks like Ned Lambert's brother, he sees the only motor car to appear in the whole of *Ulysses*.

28. James's Street. The rooftops in the foreground are those of the Guinness Brewery buildings on the south side of the street. Mr Kernan approaches from further along the street, near the church spire (which has since been truncated). Starting on the south side, he crosses soon after viewing himself in Kennedy's mirror, and walks along the sunny north side to the corner of Watling Street at the extreme right.

Walking on along the street, he looks ahead towards the site of Robert Emmet's execution, outside St Catherine's Church in Thomas Street. Emmet was twenty-five years old when he led a band of United Irishmen in an abortive rebellion in 1803. The facts of the uprising were familiar to Dubliners in 1904 after the centenary commemorations of the previous year, though Emmet's burial place is still to be established – Glasnevin, St Michan's, St Paul's and St Catherine's are among the candidates.

Opposite the top of Watling Street is the entrance to the famous Guinness Brewery, founded in 1769 by Arthur Guinness. Visitors, who no longer need to wait in the waiting room across the street, are now received in Crane Street (the next turn to the right), where the Guinness Hop Store is home to the brewery museum and the 'World of Guinness' exhibition as well as a bar serving the celebrated brew.

198   Mr Kernan, however, turns left opposite the brewery (a Guinness-sponsored plaque on the corner records the event) and walks 'down the slope of Watling street', passing the Distillery stores on the right at the corner of Bonham Street. The distillery buildings, including the prominent but sailless windmill, are now part of the Guinness complex in the middle of what has recently been designated Dublin's 'Digital Hub', an international digital enterprise area. At the time of writing there is a proposal to install a digital information centre devoted to *Ulysses* in the windmill, which will make this book, and your legs, redundant. Oblivious to such plans, Mr Kernan passes Island Street and spies the viceregal cavalcade on the far side of the river, but is too late to register his greetings.

In interpolations in this section we see Bob Cowley and Mr Dedalus meeting on Ormond Quay, the crumpled throwaway floating past North Wall and Sir John Rogerson's Quay (which appear to move westward in relation to it), and Mr and Mrs Breen walking across O'Connell Bridge en route from Bachelor's Walk to Dame Street.

Just in front of Mr Kernan is Bloody Bridge, so named after the outcome of a riot raised in support of the ferrymen whom it put out of business in 1670. The original wooden bridge was replaced in 1704 by a stone one, which was in turn succeeded by the present metal structure in 1863 under the name of Victoria Bridge. Since 1939 it has been known as Rory O'More Bridge, after the leader of the 1641 rebellion who lived nearby.

Mr Kernan's eventual destination is the Ormond Hotel on the far side of the river, though what route he takes to arrive there on p.227 is not specified. He may have crossed here at the bridge and turned right along the north quays. Before following him, turn right along the south quays on Usher's Island. Here at No. 15 is the house where the Misses Morkan held their party in 'The Dead', the last story in *Dubliners*. The top storey of the building has been removed, but the first-floor rooms, described in the story, still survive. John Huston's film of 'The Dead' (1987) used the exterior of the original building and accurate reconstructions of the interior. Left empty for some years, the house suffered at the hands of thieves and vandals, and is now in the hands of a new owner who is raising funds for a full and faithful restoration.

Return to Bloody Bridge and cross to the north quays. Turn right, and then left up Blackhall Place (directly opposite 15 Usher's Island). On the left is the 'Bluecoat School', properly King's Hospital School, built by Thomas Ivory in 1773. Students in the school, which was founded by royal charter, wore the traditional blue uniforms up to 1923. When the school moved to new premises in Palmerstown the building was acquired by the Incorporated Law Society of Ireland.

Continue up to the top of Blackhall Place to the corner on the left where Arbour Hill meets Stoney Batter. Arbour Hill, as Joyce would have known when writing *Ulysses*, had become a place of particular veneration for Irish nationalism since 1916, when the executed leaders of the Easter Rising were buried here under quicklime at the corner of the barracks, at the far end of the lane. Wolfe Tone and the Sheares brothers were also imprisoned here at the barracks in 1798.

Cyclops, 5 p.m.

240   I was just passing the time of day with old Troy of the D.M.P. at the corner of Arbour hill there . . .

The anonymous narrator of this episode – known to scholars as the Nameless One – is a 'collector of bad and doubtful debts'. He has been trying to extract money from Michael Geraghty at 29 Arbour Hill (along the road on the corner with Chicken Lane, now Ardrigh Road), when, after an unrecorded conversation with a member of the Dublin Metropolitan Police, he meets Joe Hynes coming from the City Arms Hotel at 55 Prussia Street (a former residence of the Blooms, between Stoney Batter and the North Circular Road) where he has been reporting on the cattle traders' meeting.

As the narrator explains his business to Joe, we are treated to the first of a series of interruptions in the narrative, written in a variety of 'specialist' styles according to their point of view. Thus the dispute 241 between Geraghty and Herzog is couched in legal jargon of the most pedantic variety, while the description of St Michan's Parish is in the style of neo-Celtic romantic legend.

The pair walk to Barney Kiernan's 'by the Linenhall barracks and the back of the courthouse'. To go by the barracks they would most likely have gone along North Brunswick Street (but see the *Alternative route* below), passing the Richmond Hospital on their left. Founded in 1811, the hospital was rebuilt in its present Tudor style in 1900, and since 1987 has been adapted to a new role as the Dublin Metropolitan District Courthouse.

All around them lies 'the land of holy Michan', the parish bounded by the North Circular Road, Dorset and Capel Streets and the river. It is named after St Michan's church in Church Street, with its fifteenth-century 'watchtower' and its famous vaults where bodies – some of them believed to be as much as eight hundred years old – lie preserved by the dry air, 'as in life they slept'. Among these 'warriors and princes' are the Sheares brothers, executed for their part in the 1798 rebellion,

and Lord Leitrim, a particularly hated landlord, who was
242   murdered in 1878. The 'shining palace' is the North City
Market off Chancery Street, with its stalls of fruit and
vegetables, while 'the herds innumerable' are flocking to
the Cattle Market beside the City Arms Hotel in Prussia
Street.

Beyond the Richmond Hospital and Carmichael
House next door, North Brunswick Street meets Church
Street, and originally continued on the other side where
a block of Corporation flats now stands. Cross Church
Street here, turn left up the hill and then right into
Coleraine Street which leads behind the flats. Here, rejoin
the original route by turning left into Lisburn Street. The
Linenhall barracks, which stood to the north of Lisburn
Street, were destroyed in the 1916 rebellion and have
been replaced by housing. At the end of Lisburn Street
turn right along Lurgan Street and left onto North King
Street.

Alternative route via North King Street. The above route
depends entirely on taking the phrase 'by the Linenhall
barracks' to mean that the narrator and Joe actually passed
the barrack building. On the other hand, the more direct
route from Stoney Batter to Barney Kiernan's, along
North King Street, still passes within a short distance of
the barracks, and this is possibly what the narrator may
have meant. To the right of North King Street is an
extensive cobbled area called Smithfield, the ancient
Haymarket of Dublin, traditionally known for horse
trading and recently developed as a 'civic space'. A rival
candidate for the 'watchtower' may now be the chimney
of the old Bow Street distillery which has been opened
as a viewing point.

Follow North King Street beyond Church Street and
turn right down Halston Street, past the back of Green
Street courthouse. This building, where the Central
Criminal Court is located, at that time also housed the

Recorder's Court. Robert Emmet's trial was held in the courthouse, and he and the Sheares brothers are commemorated by the monument erected in 1903 in the little park at the bottom of the street where once stood the infamous Newgate Gaol. The emotive inscription in Irish and English and the idealised figure of Erin with her wolfhound and cross reflect the character of Irish nationalism at the time. Cross the park into Green Street and cross again to the corner of Green Street and Little Britain Street. Just around the corner on the left is a hairdresser's shop at No. 9, all that remains of Barney Kiernan's pub, which also originally comprised Nos. 8 and 10.

In the pub they meet another nameless person merely referred to as 'the citizen', who is generally believed to be based on Michael Cusack, founder of the Gaelic 243 Athletic Association. Joe buys three pints of Guinness 244 with the money that he drew from the cashier in the 245 *Freeman* before lunch, and the citizen accepts the drink while reviling the *Freeman*. He also pours scorn on the *Irish Independent* for its British orientation.

'As they quaffed their cup of joy', Alf Bergan comes in and hides behind the snug. Bob Doran is discovered 'snoring drunk' in the corner; it is not clear whether or not he has visited another pub in the Liberties (the direction in which he was heading on page 202) before coming here. Alf points out through the door at Mr and Mrs Breen, who have come up from the subsheriff's office 246 to the courthouse, looking for libel action over the matter of the anonymous postcard. Alf, who works in Fanning's office, has apparently followed them up Capel Street to see the fun. He gets a 'pony' – a third of a pint of Guinness – from Terry the barman and hands over a penny in payment. Victorian pennies were, of course, common in change three years after her death, and were still in good circulation up to 1971 when old pennies became obsolete. A Joycean commentator, who shall remain appropriately nameless, interpreted the word 'testoon' as a coronation mug, involving Alf and Terry in a mysterious exchange of drinking vessels.

29. Barney Kiernan's. This is a late picture of Barney Kiernan's, where cases in the nearby Criminal Court were traditionally re-argued over a few pints.

The citizen spots Bloom 'prowling up and down 247 outside' and Alf produces some hangmen's letters. Before the others can read them, however, alarm is caused by Alf's casual remark that he saw Paddy Dignam 'not five minutes ago' in Capel Street. Joe Hynes, who saw Dignam 248 buried that morning, disillusions Alf, and Bob Doran 249 begins to weep drunkenly about Dignam. A remark by the narrator clearly identifies him with Mr Doran of 'The Boarding House' in *Dubliners*, who married his landlady's daughter.

Bloom, who has been waiting around in Green Street to meet Martin Cunningham, comes warily in past the citizen's dog and is pressed by Joe to have a drink. In the end he accepts a cigar.

The original of this episode in the *Odyssey* tells how

Ulysses and his men were captured by the Cyclops, a one-eyed giant, and kept in his cave to be eaten one by one. Ulysses plied the giant with drink, telling him his name was 'Noman', and when the Cyclops fell asleep he blinded him with a burning stick. The other giants heard the Cyclops' cries but went away when they were told 'Noman has wounded me'. Ulysses and his men escaped from the cave and taunted the giant as they sailed away. Enraged, the Cyclops hurled a huge rock after them, which fortunately missed its target.

Various elements of the story are worked into this episode – nameless people, references to blind eyes and single eyes, treating with drink and so on. The citizen's 'tunnel vision' hatred of anything that is not Irish is another form of monocularity. Bloom's cigar, of course, takes the place of Ulysses' flaming stick.

250 The hangmen's letters give rise to a conversation about capital punishment, which in turn gets the citizen going
251 on his favourite topic, great Irish nationalist heroes and
252 martyrs. Interpolated at this point is a melodramatic account of the execution of one such hero. F. L. Radford[5] has pointed out that the passage derives much from descriptions of Robert Emmet's execution, and that elements of this and some of the other interpolations in *Cyclops* can be traced to newspaper accounts of the following events in 1903: the centenary of Emmet's rising on 23 July; King Edward VII's visit to Ireland, 21 July to 1 August; the death of Pope Leo X on 20 July, his funeral and the election and coronation of his successor Pius X; and the huge demonstration on the centenary of Emmet's
253 execution, 20 September. Rumbold the executioner is named after one of Joyce's enemies, the British consul in
254 Zurich in 1917, and the hero's 'blushing bride elect' owes much to Emmet's girlfriend Sarah Curran, who married an English officer of good family two years after the execution.

255   The citizen, Bloom and Joe get talking about the Irish
language and the Gaelic League, and the citizen speaks
256 to his dog in Irish, eliciting a few growls in reply. Joe
offers to buy another round of drinks, which the citizen
257 and the Nameless One readily accept; Bloom, however,
declines, explaining that he is just waiting for Martin
Cunningham to bring him to Dignam's house. That he
has something else weighing on his mind is indicated by
his Freudian slip about 'the wife's admirers'.

258   Bob Doran passes on drunken condolences to Mrs
Dignam and leaves the pub. With the new pints the
others start talking about the foot-and-mouth disease
259 and the cattle traders' meeting. Bloom is dismayed to
hear that Nannetti is off to London, as he had hoped to
arrange with him the renewal of Keyes's advertisement.
260 Another matter dear to the citizen's heart, the revival of
Gaelic games, is discussed. Bloom attempts to put a word
in for more cosmopolitan sports like tennis but is
drowned out by the citizen's rendering of 'A Nation Once
261 Again'. The name of Blazes Boylan crops up in connection
with the boxing match which he organised; Bloom,
painfully aware that Boylan is indulging in a particular
form of athletics at that moment, tries unsuccessfully to
262 steer the conversation back to tennis. Inevitably the
forthcoming concert tour is mentioned and the narrator
notices Bloom's discomfort.

       J. J. O'Molloy and Ned Lambert enter the pub. J. J.
has now got money, apparently from Ned, for whom he
263 buys a whiskey. In return for the loan he has done Ned
a favour at the courthouse, probably, as the narrator
suspects, 'getting him off the grand jury list'. They bring
the others up to date on the Breen story, the latest news
being that Corny Kelleher has advised Breen to have the
handwriting on the postcard examined. Alf Bergan is
accused of sending the postcard, and does not altogether
264 deny it. He appears to go rather quiet when J. J. O'Molloy,

the barrister, gives his opinion that Breen has got grounds for a libel action. 'Who wants your opinion?' thinks the narrator to himself, half-expecting the lawyer to claim his 'six and eightpence' for advice. Just then the Breens pass the door again with Corny Kelleher.

265 The citizen begins to mutter about foreigners 'coming over here to Ireland filling the country with bugs', and Bloom, at whom the remark appears to be directed, pretends not to have heard. Instead he reminds Joe about the money still owed to him, 'telling him he needn't trouble about that little matter till the first but if he would just say a word to Mr Crawford'. Having lost Nannetti, he still hopes to get Myles Crawford's co-operation in the renewal of the ad.

266 The citizen, still trying to provoke Bloom, mentions the affair between Dermot MacMurrough and Dervorgilla which first brought 'the Saxon robbers' to Ireland. Alf and Terry are giggling over a modern-day adulteress in the *Police Gazette*.

'So anyhow in came John Wyse Nolan and Lenehan with him with a face on him as long as a late breakfast.' Nolan has been at the meeting about the Irish language in City Hall; Lenehan, who was last seen leaving the Ormond Hotel at four o'clock, has met him on the way somewhere, having also found out the result of the Gold 267 Cup race. Throwaway, the outsider, has come first and his own tip, Sceptre, is 'still running'. The citizen, meanwhile, is holding forth about Ireland's great 268 resources and her opportunities for trade, ruined by 'the yellowjohns of Anglia'. He looks forward to the day when Ireland will be a nation once again.

269 John Wyse Nolan orders a 'half one...and a hands up' for himself and Lenehan, which Terry correctly interprets as a 'small whisky and a bottle of Allsop'. It will have been noticed by now that none of the drinkers ever orders a drink by its proper name; this is typical of the

innuendo and inferential language in which the entire
270 episode is written. Encouraged by the others, the citizen
inveighs against the Royal Navy and the British Empire
'of drudges and whipped serfs'. Bloom's protest 'Isn't
discipline the same everywhere?' is ignored as the others
hurl abuse at the British and their European neighbours.
271 Joe buys a third pint for the narrator and the citizen,
who show no sign of returning the favour.

Bloom, goaded into losing his cool, tries to speak out
against persecution and 'national hatred among nations',
272 but gets laughed at. His claim to be Irish elicits an
273 expressive spit from the citizen, and he lacks the eloq-
uence to make his point that life is about love instead of
hatred. Suddenly he breaks off and leaves the pub to see
if Martin Cunningham is at the courthouse.

274 The others settle back to their drinks and the citizen
reads them a skit from the *United Irishman*. Then
Lenehan leaps to a conclusion. '—Bloom, says he. The
courthouse is a blind. He had a few bob on *Throwaway*
and he's gone to gather in the shekels.'

275 The narrator goes out the back to consider this information while relieving himself. He has already consumed
two of the three pints Joe has bought him, and another
one cadged off an unnamed person earlier in Slattery's
(Suffolk House in Suffolk Street), and has a good load
to let off.

Back inside, John Wyse Nolan is claiming that Bloom
has been working behind the scenes with Arthur Griffith,
leader of the Sinn Fein nationalist movement. Martin
Cunningham arrives on the castle car with Jack Power
276 and Crofton, an 'orangeman' or loyalist who appears in
'Ivy Day in the Committee Room' in *Dubliners*. Crofton,
whose politics would normally put him in opposition to
the citizen, sides with the others in denouncing Bloom.
277 Even the reasonable Martin Cunningham fails to defuse
their hatred.

Ned Lambert buys drinks for the three new arrivals
278 and Martin Cunningham's toast 'God bless all here'
prompts an interpolation describing an enormous
procession of saints marching across the city to bless the
279 pub. The narrator, having almost finished his pint, is
looking around in hopes of being offered another one
when Bloom returns. Martin Cunningham, aware of the
ugly mood in the pub, quickly gathers his party onto the
280 jaunting car outside the door. The citizen, with Joe and
Alf trying to hold him back, staggers after them and
shouts '—Three cheers for Israel!' attracting the attention
of 'all the ragamuffins and sluts of the nation'. Bloom
stands up on the car and boldly retorts '—Your God was
281 a jew. Christ was a jew like me.' The citizen grabs the
empty biscuit-tin from the pub and hurls it after Bloom,
but as his target is heading into the sun he is, like the
Cyclops, blinded and causes no injury. An interpolation,
282 however, describes the impact as cataclysmic, leaving in
ruins the courthouse and all surrounding buildings.

283   The car gathers speed and is last seen heading southwards down Little Green Street past Donohoe's pub
(which was on the right opposite where Keeling's
warehouse now stands) 'like a shot off a shovel'.

Bloom now travels to Sandymount, probably via
Arran Street, the north quays, O'Connell Bridge and
back along the funeral route to 9 Newbridge Avenue.

At the east end of Little Britain Street is Capel Street,
where three alternatives present themselves.

A. Turn left and follow Capel Street into Bolton Street.
On the left is Henrietta Street, leading to the King's Inns
where Chandler works in 'A Little Cloud' in *Dubliners*.
Bolton Street continues into Dorset Street, leading to
Eccles Street (Tour 3).

B. Turn right along Capel Street and left along Mary
Street. On the right is St Mary's Church, founded in
1627 and recently turned into a shop. Richard Brinsley

Sheridan, Wolfe Tone and Sean O'Casey were among those baptised here. Nearly opposite at No. 45, now the east end of Penney's department store, was the Volta Cinema, which was opened by James Joyce in 1909 and closed in 1948. Follow Mary Street and Henry Street to O'Connell Street for Tour 6.

C. Turn right and follow Capel Street to the quays near the Ormond Hotel, and across the river up Parliament Street and Cork Hill to Dublin Castle for Tour 5.

Notes

[1] 'The Best Recent Scholarship in Joyce,' Danis Rose, *James Joyce Quarterly*, vol. 23, no. 3 (1986).

[2] *Bloomsday: The Eleventh Hour – A Quest for the Vacant Place* (A Wake Newslitter Press, 1981).

[3] 'The Discovery of *Ruby*', Mary Power, *James Joyce Quarterly*, vol. 18, no. 2 (1981).

[4] Bruce Bidwell and Linda Heffer: *The Joycean Way – A Topographic Guide to Dubliners and A Portrait of the Artist as a Young Man* (Wolfhound Press, 1981).

[5] King, Pope and Hero-Martyr: *Ulysses* and the Nightmare of Irish History', F.L. Radford, *James Joyce Quarterly*, vol. 15, no. 4 (1978).

Photograph Reference Numbers

Photograph number **3.** R1114; **4.** R10963; **6.** IMP 750; **7.** R725; **8.** R1189; **9.** R10309; **10.** R1095; **11.** R4067; **12.** R711; **13.** IMP2293; **14.** R1197; **16.** R1650; **17.** R5941; **18.** IMP2517; **20.** NS5383; **21.** IMP494; **22.** NS5388; **23.** NS5173; **24.** R702; **25.** R672; **26.** R1655; **27.** R969

The index numbers refer to photographs in the Lawrence Collection of the National Library of Ireland, held at the National Photographic Archive.

Appendix 1 *The Movements of Leopold Bloom and Stephen Dedalus on 16 June 1904*

LEOPOLD BLOOM

8.00–8.45 a.m. *Calypso*:
7 Eccles Street and Dlugacz's.

8.45–9.45 a.m. Eccles Street to Sir John Rogerson's Quay.

9.45–10.30 a.m. *Lotuseaters*:
Sir John Rogerson's Quay to Lincoln Place.

10.30–11.00 a.m. Leinster Street baths; Sandymount tram to Haddington Road and Newbridge Avenue.

11.00 a.m.–12.15 p.m. *Hades*:
Sandymount to Glasnevin. Coaches return mourners to city centre.

12.15–1.10 p.m. *Aeolus*:
Newspaper office; visits Keyes in Bachelor's Walk and returns.

1.10–2.10 p.m. *Laestrygonians*:
Abbey Street to Kildare Street via Davy Byrne's.

2.10–2.55 p.m. *Scylla and Charybdis*:
National Museum, National Library.

STEPHEN DEDALUS

8.00–8.45 a.m. *Telemachus*:
Joyce Tower and Forty Foot.

8.45–9.45 a.m. Joyce Tower to Mr Deasy's school; lesson starting 9.00 a.m.

9.45–10.05 a.m. *Nestor*:
Mr Deasy's school, Summerfield, Dalkey Avenue.

10.05–10.40 a.m. Dalkey to Sandymount via Lansdowne Road station.

10.40–11.10 a.m. *Proteus*:
Sandymount Strand. Ringsend to Irishtown.

11.10 a.m.–12.15 p.m. Walks into town along funeral route. Visits College Green P.O.

12.15–1.10 p.m. *Aeolus*:
Newspaper office; across O'Connell Street to Mooney's in Abbey Street.

1.10–2.10 p.m. Drinking in Mooney's *en ville* (Abbey Street) and *sur mer* (now the Horse and Tram on Eden Quay); proceeds to National Library, probably by same route as Bloom.

2.10–2.55 p.m. *Scylla and Charybdis*:
National Library.

2.55–3.40 p.m. *Wandering Rocks*:
From National Library to Bedford
Row, Merchant's Arch and Wellington
Quay.

2.55–3.40 p.m. *Wandering Rocks*:
Walks to the front gate of Trinity College and meets Almidano Artifoni. Continues to Fleet Street and Bedford Row.

3.40–4.30 p.m. *Sirens*:
Wellington Quay to the Ormond
Hotel, and thence to Marks's on
Ormond Quay.

3.40 p.m. onwards. Spent some or all
of the next six hours drinking in the
Moira, 15 Trinity Street, and
Larchet's, 11 College Green, eventually reaching Holles Street hospital
with the medical students.

4.30–5.45 p.m. *Cyclops*:
Via Chancery Street, Greek Street,
Mary's Lane and Little Green Street
to Barney Kiernan's in Little Britain
Street.

5.45–6.00 p.m. By jaunting car from
Barney Kiernan's via (probably) Little
Green Street, Arran Street, north
quays, O'Connell Bridge, D'Olier
Street and Brunswick (Pearse) Street
to 9 Newbridge Avenue.

6.00–8.25 p.m. 9 Newbridge Avenue,
and thence to Sandymount Strand via
Leahy's Terrace.

8.25–9.00 p.m. *Nausikaa*:
Sandymount Strand.

9.00–10.00 p.m. Sandymount Strand,
and thence by tram to Holles Street
Hospital.

10.00–11.15 p.m. *Oxen of the Sun*:
Holles Street Hospital, and thence to
Burke's pub and via Denzille Lane to
Westland Row.
11.15–11.35 p.m. Westland Row
Station to Killester Station and back
to Amiens Street Station.

10.00–11.15 p.m. *Oxen of the Sun*:
Holles Street Hospital, Burke's pub to
Westland Row.

11.15 – 11.25 p.m. Westland Row
Station to Amiens Street Station.

11.35 p.m.–12.40 a.m. *Circe*:
Amiens Street, Talbot Street, Mabbot
Street, Bella Cohen's in Tyrone Street,
and Beaver Street.

11.25 p.m. –12.40 a.m. *Circe*:
Amiens Street to Bella Cohen's and
Beaver Street.

12.40–1.00 a.m. *Eumaeus*:
Beaver Street to Amiens Street, Store
Street and Butt Bridge.

12.40–1.00 a.m. *Eumaeus*:
Beaver Street to Amiens Street, Store
Street and Butt Bridge.

1.00–2.00 a.m. *Ithaca*:
Butt Bridge to Gardiner Street,
Gardiner Place, North Temple Street
and 7 Eccles Street.

1.00–2.00 a.m. *Ithaca*:
Butt Bridge to 7 Eccles Street, and
thence into the unknown.

2.00 a.m. onwards. *Penelope*:
Asleep in 7 Eccles Street.

Appendix II Ulysses: *The Corrected Text*

The text to which this guide refers is the 1986 edition of *Ulysses*, known as 'The
Corrected Text', which laid down a standard text with identical lines and page
numbers in all British and American editions, hardback and paperback.

The 'corrected' edition was made necessary by the fact that every single previous edition contained large quantities of typographical errors, omissions and
unintended variations overlooked at the time of the original publication in
1922 and subsequently perpetuated. The task was not just a simple one of referring to the original manuscript of the novel, since Joyce made substantial revi-
sions and additions on typescripts and several sets of proofs, amounting to
approximately 25 per cent of the final text. The combination of an American
publisher, a French printer and typesetter, and typists of various nationalities,
all trying to interpret the difficult handwriting and unpredictable syntax of a
half-blind Irish genius, was only part of the story.

The editors of the 1986 edition, in their search for an 'ideal' text, had to
spend seven years collating and assessing every known variation on the text of
Ulysses that could be attributed to Joyce himself. In several cases there was no clear
preference between two or more readings and the judgement had to rest on editorial discretion. Few of the more than five thousand alterations to established
texts, however, make any great difference to the interpretation of the novel. Most
of them are based on punctuation and minor spelling differences, but in some
cases phrases and even whole sentences have been restored. Richard Ellmann dis-
cusses some of the more interesting corrections in his introduction to the text.

The credibility of the Corrected Text, however, came under sustained attack from critics who disagreed with its editorial principles, and it is now regarded as no more definitive than its predecessors. As a substantially 'new' text it remained in copyright when the older editions passed into the public domain in 1992 (confusingly, due to a change in copyright laws, they have since gone back into copyright) and were widely reissued in popular reprints which knocked the Corrected Text out of the market. Today's reader is just as likely to be using a facsimile of the 1922 first edition, or a text based on the Bodley Head edition of 1960, or even the controversial 'Reader's Edition' of 1997 in which the text was not only corrected but also copy-edited to bring Joyce into line with conventional spelling and punctuation.

By general consensus the Corrected Text remains the standard for reference purposes, and the page numbers in the margins of this guide refer to that edition. For those using other editions, the quotations in the Guide may be used as signposts to help locate the corresponding pages in the copy of *Ulysses* in hand.

Appendix III *Joyce's Schema and the Episode Titles*

In 1921 Joyce lent Carlo Linati a schema or plan of *Ulysses* in which he assigned to each episode a title from an episode in Homer's *Odyssey*, a time, a colour, persons, a technique, a science or art, a sense or meaning, an organ of the body and a symbol. Joyce also lent it to Valery Larbaud for a lecture, in order, as he said, 'to help him to confuse the audience a little more'. In 1931 Joyce allowed Stuart Gilbert to publish most of the schema in *James Joyce's Ulysses*, with a number of changes (suggesting that parts of the plan were made to fit the book rather than the other way round). The full text of both versions is reproduced in Richard Ellmann's *Ulysses by the Liffey*.

The information contained in the schema does not convey much in the way of clarification. However, it is referred to occasionally in the Guide where it seems of particular interest. Some of the times given in the plan are misleading, and Joyce himself changed his mind about the times of the later episodes in the second version of the schema. The times quoted in the Guide are taken from the schema only when internal evidence does not suggest otherwise.

The Homeric titles given to the episodes are traditionally used by commentators, although they do not appear in the text of *Ulysses*. Joyce did use them in early drafts and later dropped them, but gave his approval for Stuart Gilbert and Frank Budgen to use the titles in their books. The spelling of some of the Greek names varies according to the commentator.

Bibliography

Bruce Bidwell and Linda Heffer, *The Joycean Way: A Topographic Guide to Dubliners and A Portrait of the Artist as a Young Man*, Wolfhound Press, 1981.

Harry Blamires, *The Bloomsday Book*, Methuen, 1966.

Carole Brown and Leo Knuth, *Bloomsday: The Eleventh Hour – A Quest for the Vacant Place*, A Wake Newslitter Press, 1981.

Frank Budgen, *James Joyce and the Making of Ulysses*, Grayson and Grayson, 1934.

Desmond Clarke, *Dublin*, Batsford, 1977.

Maurice Craig, *Dublin, 1660-1860*, Hodges Figgis, 1952.

Frank Delaney, *James Joyce's Odyssey*, Hodder and Stoughton, 1981.

Richard Ellmann, *James Joyce* (revised edition), Oxford University Press, 1982.

—*Ulysses on the Liffey*, Faber and Faber, 1972.

—*James Joyce's Tower*, Eastern Regional Tourism Organisation, 1969.

Stuart Gilbert, *James Joyce's Ulysses: A Study*, Faber and Faber, 1930.

Oliver St John Gogarty, *It Isn't This Time of Year at All!*, MacGibbon and Kee, 1954.

Clive Hart and Leo Knuth, *A Topographical Guide to James Joyce's Ulysses* (revised and corrected edition), A Wake Newslitter Press, 1981.

James Joyce, *Ulysses: The Corrected Text*, Penguin Books/The Bodley Head, 1986.

—*Dubliners: The Corrected Text*, Jonathan Cape, 1967.

—*A Portrait of the Artist as a Young Man*, B. W. Huebsch, 1916.

—*Letters of James Joyce, Vol. I* (ed. Stuart Gilbert), Faber and Faber, 1957.

—*Letters of James Joyce, Vol. II and III* (ed. Richard Ellmann), Faber and Faber, 1966.

Weston St John Joyce, *The Neighbourhood of Dublin*, 1912 (revised edition, 1922, Gill).

Pat Liddy, 'Dublin Today', *Irish Times*.

Frank MacDonald, *The Destruction of Dublin*, Gill and Macmillan, 1985.

Frederick O'Dwyer, *Lost Dublin*, Gill and Macmillan, 1981.

Mary Power, 'The Discovery of *Ruby*,' *James Joyce Quarterly*, Vol. 18, No. 2, 1981.

F. L. Radford, 'King, Pope and Hero-Martyr: Ulysses and the Nightmare of Irish History', *James Joyce Quarterly*, Vol. 15, No. 4, 1978.

Danis Rose, 'The Best Recent Scholarship in Joyce', *James Joyce Quarterly*, Vol. 23, No. 3, 1986.

Weldon Thornton, *Allusions in Ulysses: An Annotated List*, University of North Carolina Press, 1968.

Mervyn Wall, *Forty Foot Gentlemen Only*, Allen Figgis, 1962.

Note: This bibliography is not an exhaustive one. Essentially it is a list of those works consulted or cited specifically in connection with the writing of this book. There are, of course, many other books on Joyce and on Dublin which have contributed to my views and knowledge of the subject over a period of years.

Index

Index • 169